Intensive English

Higher Intermediate Level

Teacher's Book

Meg Tafner
Tony Williams

REGENT SCHOOL OF ENGLISH
19-23 Oxford Street, London W1R 1RF
Telephone: 01-734 7455

MACMILLAN
PUBLISHERS

© Text Meg Tafner and Tony Williams 1988
© Illustrations Macmillan Publishers Limited 1988

All rights reserved. No reproduction, copy or transmission of this publication may be made without written permission. No paragraph of this publication may be reproduced, copied or transmitted save with written permission or in accordance with the provisions of the Copyright Act 1956 (as amended). Any person who does any unauthorised act in relation to this publication may be liable to criminal prosecution and civil claims for damages.

First published 1988

Published by *Macmillan Publishers Ltd*
London and Basingstoke
*Associated Companies and Representatives in Accra,
Auckland, Delhi, Dublin, Gaborone, Hamburg, Harare,
Hong Kong, Kuala Lumpur, Lagos, Manzini, Melbourne,
Mexico City, Nairobi, New York, Singapore, Tokyo*

Typeset by Katerprint Typesetting Services, Oxford

Printed in Hong Kong

British Library Cataloguing in Publication Data
Tafner, Meg
  Intensive English
  Higher intermediate level
  Teacher's bk
  1. English language—Text-books for
  foreign speakers
  I. Title   II. Williams, Tony
  428.2′4   PE1128

ISBN 0-333-42090-X

Contents

Introduction	page iv
Unit 1	1
Unit 2	6
Unit 3	10
Unit 4	12
Unit 5	15
Unit 6	18
Unit 7	19
Unit 8	22
Unit 9	24
Unit 10	27
Unit 11	30
Unit 12	32
Unit 13	35
Unit 14	39
Unit 15	41
Unit 16	43
Unit 17	46
Unit 18	48
Unit 19	50
Unit 20	52
Listening scripts	54

Introduction

Intensive English is a topic-based short course designed for learners wishing to improve their active use and understanding of English at higher intermediate level.

Topics

The material, mostly authentic but also in part specially written, is aimed at young adult and adult students. It is designed to be entertaining without being either trivial or condescending. From their own experience, the authors understand that material which is somewhat out of the ordinary is most likely to gain and hold the attention and interest of the learner. While *Intensive English* takes account of the pop sub-culture of the young it does not pander to this. The authors know that while many young people are interested in rock music, clothes and so on, these same people can be equally passionate about problems of the day. The environment, for example – the Chernobyl disaster – is the focus for one unit; ecology – the problems of ecological living – provides the topic for another.

Other topics concern relationships: with each other, as friends, before and during marriage, with the roles of parents and children, and as prospective parents. Students may be deeply concerned about job prospects, and the quality of life both out of work and in it. They are also, of course, concerned with health, sport, challenge and adventure, personal success. All these are taken up in *Intensive English*.

The topics covered in the course are not culture-specific or Anglocentric. The assumption is that it is English *language* the learners want to acquire and not the English or British way of life, and if they learn something about the English themselves, then this is incidental to the main purpose. The reading and listening materials involve or concern people of different nationalities who describe many experiences and even fears with which we can all in some way identify. When travelling away from home, for example, in a strange country or city, a constant fear is that of getting lost or being late – a theme taken up in the story of the Bull Ring, which is set in Birmingham but could equally well happen in a score of modern cities.

Problems of our time, such as immigration or finding and keeping work, the position of women in work and the outcome of the 'Decade for Women' also provide a rich source of topics. These and similar issues, which provide the backbone of the course, are treated sympathetically, though never with a polemic voice – a serious look at the problem of food additives is matched by a light-hearted item on a new method of caviar production, for example.

Since the selected topics have an obvious bearing on their lives and situations, learners are more inclined to use them as a springboard for discussion and project work inside and outside the classroom. They are designed to generate the maximum opportunity for meaningful communication together with the integration and improvement of all the skills involved in learning a language.

The units have not been graded in order of difficulty. The course has been assembled so that a unit can be selected either because the topic is relevant to current class-work or because it reflects the interests and needs of the students themselves.

Structure and use of units

Each unit, apart from Unit 10 which has no Listening section, consists of listening material (recorded on the accompanying cassette) and reading texts; these have been taken from many sources – short stories, newspaper articles, radio interviews and personal accounts.

Group and pair work is an essential part of the exploitation of the materials. Each unit contains suggestions for written work and vocabulary expansion. Grammar points arising from the unit are explained and practised separately. This means that the course is flexible enough to allow parts to be extracted and worked on separately without affecting the course as a whole.

The Diary at the end of each unit is to be completed by each student as a personal assessment record. It is designed to encourage honest self-evaluation so that the learner can pinpoint problems and outline progress for each unit. Teachers should inspect the Diary regularly and discuss it with the student. Additional practice material can then be set to give specific help to the individual.

Teacher's Notes

The Teacher's Notes for Unit 1 have been written in greater detail to provide a model for the suggested exploitation of other units. While not all the suggested activities or approaches are suitable for every unit, most provide a basis for adaptation.

Teacher's Notes for the remainder of the units are given in less detail. They do provide answers to the Students' Book tasks, some notes on points of difficulty in texts, plus additional exercises and vocabulary work to supplement the Students' Book. Listening scripts are provided in full.

Suggestions for dealing with reading

Each unit of *Intensive English* includes a reading text which is central to the topic focus of the unit. The type and style of the text varies considerably throughout the course as do the activities based on it.

Pre-Reading

Before looking at any text with the class, the teacher should be familiar with the topic in general and the text in particular. Pre-reading tasks, questions, pictures for discussion are essential in order to get the most out of the reading by encouraging the students to start thinking along certain lines. Draw up a list of questions which will lead into the subject matter of the reading material and stimulate interest. Collect any pictorial material which can be used to build relevant vocabulary or lead into a brief discussion. Refer to the short vocabulary check before each text (where none appears in the Students' Book, please refer to the Teacher's Notes) or, alternatively, deal with key vocabulary during the pre-reading activities.

Reading

There are several approaches to the reading of a text:
- It can be read aloud by the teacher while the students follow.
- It can be read silently by individual students.
- It can be read aloud to the class by a selection of student readers.
- It can be prepared in advance by the student working at home.
- It can be read aloud by some or all of the members of a small reading/study group.

There is no right way or wrong way to organise reading activities. Of course, a varied approach is the most desirable, but the choice has to depend upon the feelings of the teacher and the class.

The texts themselves are designed to be read in several ways, including:
- reading for information/background data
- scanning for specific items
- reading for comprehension
- skimming for gist
- reading a specific section of text in order to pass on information in an oral report.

Exploitation

The exercises which follow the text are designed to check the reader's understanding of:
- content/information, either general or specific
- lexical items
- identification of key points
- certain linguistic features.

These exercises are probably best tackled by small groups, then checked through by the teacher with the whole class together.

Following each text is also a list of points for discussion. These are designed to draw out the knowledge and opinion of the student. Many students are reluctant to voice opinions to the whole class, so working in small groups is again recommended. The discussion guidelines, it is hoped, will provide the chance for all members of the group to make a contribution. Cross-group reporting accompanied by some note-taking should then take place, so that comparisons can be made of the different or similar directions taken by the work of each group.

Suggestions for dealing with listening

Each unit of *Intensive English* has recorded material for listening practice. The interviews are based on actual recordings made 'in the field' and are presented in a variety of accents. The contents have been recorded at normal speaking speed, as the authors believe there is nothing to be gained from slowing down or in any other way simplifying what is usually heard in an English-speaking context.

Preparation

Whether the material is heard by an individual (in a language laboratory) or a small group from the class, or by the whole class at once, it is most important to prepare the listener properly. Many listening sections in the Students' Book have lists of key words which need to be understood before the tape is played. (Where no list appears in the Students' Book, please refer to the Teacher's Notes.) It is equally important that the listener is prepared for listening by being asked to think about or comment on certain issues or questions on the topic content of the recording.

Reading through the comprehension questions on the listening piece is another means whereby students can get an idea of the content of the recording and also be quite clear about what information they need to listen for.

Presentation

In the language laboratory or the classroom, once the preparatory work has been completed, it is recommended that the listening passage is played once in its entirety. Questions on gist are a useful way to assess how much information has been absorbed.

Play the tape a second time, either with or without pauses, for checking questions, depending upon the ability of the student group. It is always useful to get the students to take a few notes while listening. These can be of a general nature or related to the set questions. Parts of the tape which present problems for the students can be played in isolation for intensive listening, or used as a 'listen and repeat' exercise.

Listen to the material a third time in order to check students' notes or answers, or to provide another chance to catch something that hasn't been fully grasped or understood.

Exploitation

Before asking students to volunteer answers, it is often helpful to allow them to compare notes, thus providing another opportunity for speaking.

Follow-up work is just as important as preparatory work. The word list at the beginning may be used again to check memory, comprehension, spelling, putting words into sentences etc.

Some discussion of the answers is also most desirable, again providing chances for students to practise speaking, use new vocabulary, air their views on the topic or volunteer further information.

Suggestions for dealing with discussion

A central feature in the design of the course is the importance attached to discussion and debate inside and outside the classroom.

Some suggestions on how to set up and manage discussions are given in the Teacher's Notes for Unit 1. A basic approach is to divide the class into working groups and give each one a small information-gathering project (in Unit 18 for instance, to go to a local supermarket and note down all the additives listed on a selection of pre-packaged, processed foods). Each group then collates its results and a speaker reports its findings to the class. The whole class then debates its opinions on the issues raised.

Another approach used throughout the course is the pre-reading or pre-listening discussion. Guided questions help students who may be less likely to have any pre-formed views, or who may be too shy to volunteer opinions, but who will work with guidelines. Later, groups can be asked to say how their views have or have not been modified in the light of what they have read, listened to, or gleaned from other class members. This can be done more formally by taking a vote on an issue.

The teacher can assume a more or less active role – setting class assignments, dividing the class into discussion groups, correcting spoken errors where appropriate and offering individual encouragement and advice. The degree of involvement of the teacher depends to some extent on the personality or composition of the group and will vary from class to class, but should at least involve the monitoring of each working group.

Role play

Role play exercises which appear in many of the units are designed to give the learner further opportunities for practising certain structures dealt with in the unit. Students may enjoy being able to set up their own role play situations. Some interesting and valuable work may be created in this way, particularly if a small group formulates a set of characters within a situation, then gives the acting-out task to another group in the class.

Unit 1

Opening discussion

Students cover the names of the buildings and guess what each of the drawings might be.

Keeping the names covered, feed a selection of buildings to the class in random order. Ask if they can describe what they think a terraced house, for example, looks like.

Students uncover the names and, working in pairs, match the names with the pictures.

Answer key
a) cottage
c) terraced house
f) chalet
g) bungalow
d) detached house
h) farm
b) semi-detached house
e) mansion

To follow the matching exercise, the teacher can set this optional pair-work exercise.

Design a layout: introduce the exercise by showing students a floor plan of the building where you work. Set a time limit of about 10 minutes. Students in pairs should choose one of the homes illustrated and do a very quick sketch of a floor plan for it. The time limit is important. The design and furnishing of the individual rooms may also be considered if time allows.

Give the class these instructions:

Working with a partner, choose *one* of these homes and plan the layout as if you had unlimited funds and could design the property from scratch. Make your description as interesting as possible and present your plan to the rest of the class, who must then decide whether or not it would be possible or desirable to give you permission to build it.

This lends itself to some vocabulary-checking for knowledge, pronunciation, etc.

Vocabulary areas include *location* words, eg adjacent, adjoining, opposite, next to; *design* and *style* words, eg Georgian, Tudor, Victorian, modern, post-war, formal, open-plan.

The students ought to discuss town planning in small groups – pool knowledge of their own personal area regulations or decide what might be appropriate for the area near the school. Then the plans/ presentations can be examined in that light, and a vote taken.

Reading

Text: 'Computer Home on the Way'
Before looking at the text, elicit students' ideas on what the homes of

the future might be like, and how they will differ from the homes of today. This is a good way to encourage some vocabulary-building in preparation for the news article. Think about the ways in which modern technology has already made changes in our homes.

Guess the meaning of the words in the list above the text and follow with some dictionary checking. A time limit of about five minutes should be set.

Reading activity

See suggestions on page vi.

Check your understanding

Answer key
1 In ten years, within the next decade
2 A rapid rise or upsurge in sales
3 The computer will play a vital role channelling information to and from the world outside and also controlling devices in the home.
4 Cable television signals are carried directly into the home by a wire and not sent over the airwaves.
5 Shops are linked to a local bank in a network enabling shoppers to buy goods without using money or writing cheques.

Class activity

The role of the chairperson is to maintain order. We suggest the teacher takes this role in the first instance. Each speaker should have an assistant to help with the presentation of a brief argument for or against the motion. After these presentations, which must not be interrupted, the chairperson declares the debate 'open to the floor'. Individuals chosen by the chairperson may then offer comments or opinions one at a time without being interrupted.

An open vote by show of hands is taken at the end.

Writing

Before the debate, suggest that students take notes on what is said. Group work to follow will lead to an exchange of ideas and information. Choose some copies of a local newspaper to get an idea of style and presentation. Think of a headline for the article. Students can work either alone or with a partner.

Listening

Pre-listening suggestion

Elicit from the students their ideas on how an ideal world should be organised in order to maintain a good ecological balance. Steer the discussion towards the perfect ecological house, and ask for ideas about building materials, power for heating and lighting, recycling of materials, etc. Include some new vocabulary (see listening script on p. 54) from the recording.

Listening and note-taking can be done individually, either in the classroom or in the language laboratory. Play the tape at least twice (see Introduction, p. vii). Notes should be made under the given headings. Students can check with a partner to compare how much information they were able to take down while listening.

Answer key
1 I didn't really like it, I couldn't settle down in the city.
2 We were re-decorating, improving the building.
3 Rabbits were re-establishing themselves, returning (after the myxomatosis epidemic in the 1950s, which wiped out almost the entire rabbit population of Britain).
4 We employed, engaged, commissioned architects.
5 The ecology idea was just taking off, first becoming popular.
6 Allow, enable the sunlight to (shine on), reach the house
7 The pit emitted, produced gas.
8 My husband left me.

Additional material

The following gap-fill exercise is useful for revision of the unit, or can alternatively be used as further practice material.

We suggest that the text be copied on to an acetate sheet for use with an overhead projector. The correct words should be shuffled and included with another 12–15 distractors in a box at the bottom of the sheet. This kind of activity is usually best done in pairs or small groups.

The following is a passage from which all the prepositions have been removed. Try to supply them.

The world is looking _____ a fuel crisis of disastrous proportions. But not yet. For the moment the earth is still bulging _____ coal waiting to be won, _____ the sea and the land oil is waiting to be pumped _____. But man seems to be intent only _____ using these resources _____. With an amazing recklessness he works _____ this generation alone, forgetting all _____ the needs _____ his grandchildren. Ignoring the more friendly energy providers, the wind, sun and waves, he goes _____ the easiest road, digging _____ the coal and pumping oil _____ beneath the ground.

Answer key
1 at
2 with
3 under/beneath
4 out/up
5 on
6 up
7 for
8 about
9 of
10 along
11 up
12 from

4 Intensive English
GRAMMAR GUIDE
Uses of the Future

Future simple

There is often more than one way to talk about the Future. The guidelines in the book are just that – only a guide.

As a general introduction, elicit ideas from the students about the world of tomorrow, eg what homes, clothes, transport, food, communications will be like. This can be done either by getting contributions from the whole class or (perhaps more productively) from students in smaller groups, making lists under the headings suggested above plus others that they suggest. This will provide ready material for sentence practice using the Future Simple, for use with the list of verbs most commonly used to introduce assumptions about the future.

Some examples:
I hope that the traffic will not be too noisy.
I assume that there will be enough sunlight to heat the house.
The local farmers feel sure that the eco-house will fail.
Do you suppose that the house will interfere with the local wildlife?

Present simple

Plans could include:
- a military operation, eg moving valuable equipment by air from one base to another with precise timing
- a plan for a jewellery-shop robbery
- a plan for a surprise party for someone
- a plan of action for a camping/activity weekend for 30 people.

Present continuous

Other suggestions: Working in pairs, take it in turns to choose one of the plans above. Imagine you are one of the people actually involved. Make a short list of the arrangements and their timing. Tell your partner about them.

Going to

Students in small groups can discuss their long-term plans eg jobs, further education, travelling, then each can tell the whole class two plans of two other students.

Answer key
The plumber is going to fix the toilet.
We are going to paint the house this weekend.
We are going to have to replace the glass.
The plumber is going to mend the tap.
We're going to remove the rust.
They are going to replace the bulb.
The mechanic is going to repair the indicator.

I am going to buy new tyres.
He is going to balance the wheels.

Vocabulary practice

Answer key
1   uninteresting   incomplete   uneconomic
    impossible   inappropriate   impermissible
    unnatural   unpopular   unembarrassed
    inefficient   undesirable   impolite
2   Note: Equally acceptable alternatives are shown in brackets.
    ideal (future)   cottage (house)   much   beams   up
    down   range (fire)   panel   roof   fuel (s)   glazing   out
    gas   pit   do up   fetching (bringing, carrying)

Unit 2

Reading

Answer key
1. expatriate: a person who lives abroad for an extended period
   boisterous: lively and noisy
   a glazed look: an incomprehending, expressionless look
   hauled out: took out, produced
   turned off: repelled by
   a nasal twang: an unpleasant way of singing through the nose
   cup of tea: something one likes
   for my sins: an expression used when we regret having to say or do something
   belt out a song: sing boisterously
   it dawned on me: I realised
2. The most likely answer is (b).
3. A folk singer
4. A folk song is part of the ethnic music of many countries; rock music is derived from American rhythm and blues and jazz.
5. A hotel provides full meals and room service; a boarding house usually provides only breakfast and an evening meal.
6. ... I gave way.
7. Because he was ashamed of his performance.
8. An expatriate lives abroad for an extended period. A student is not normally an expatriate.

Listening

Answer key

1	work	11	don't	21	rivers
2	before	12	goes down	22	soon
3	case	13	o'clock	23	phone
4	by	14	else	24	friends
5	this	15	the summer	25	invite
6	in	16	almost	26	start
7	face	17	heat	27	go
8	because	18	rains	28	again
9	anybody	19	lot	29	get
10	this	20	there		

Further practice

After listening to the song, get students to discuss the following questions in small groups.

1 Do you get, or have you ever been, homesick?
2 How do you imagine it makes people feel?
3 Can you suggest ways of getting over it?

GRAMMAR GUIDE

Indirect or reported speech

Answer key
1 a Joe said that her work wasn't as good as it had been.
  b She said that they had been in the waiting room for ages.
  c Martha would be leaving the house at six o'clock and could put the spare key under the flower pot.
  d Everyone had been to the party and it had been great fun.
2 a Elisabeth said to John that if he told her what was needed she could get it for him.
  b Sarah told Tom that their new house was wonderful and that he should (must) come and see them soon.
  c Eva told Christian that he could take her car if he promised to be back not later than nine o'clock.
  d She/he said they thought that they should both go on holiday.
  e Robert said that he was hoping that Anna could help him.
3 a She said that she really wanted the work to be done that day, not the day after.
  b They had left several months before but they planned to be back the following year.
  c Those books had to be sent back the next (following) day.
  d There was a very good discothèque there, and they could go either that night or the following Friday.

Further practice

Answer key
1 She suggested { that they should go / going } to the new Indian restaurant that night.
2 She insisted { that they should come and have / on their coming and having } dinner with her.
3 He invited him/her/them to join a group of them at the football match that Thursday.
4 He warned them that if they wanted tickets for the following week's show they had better book then.
5 She advised him/her to go to the police immediately and tell them everything.

Additional material

Students can practice Reported Speech by working in groups of three on the following role play exercise.
Your Great Aunt Maud is almost stone deaf.
She wants to buy a new radio-cassette player as a gift for her grandchild and has asked you to go to the shop with her . . .

8 Intensive English

SHOP ASSISTANT
Greet your customers

ASSISTANT
Offer a radio-cassette player (£60)

AUNT MAUD
You want to know what he said

AUNT MAUD
Tell them it's too expensive

AUNT
Tell your nephew that you didn't hear what the assistant said

ASSISTANT
Agree with the nephew. Show another radio-cassette

NEPHEW/NIECE
Report what the assistant said

NEPHEW/NIECE
Explain that your aunt wants to buy a good quality radio-cassette

NEPHEW/NIECE
Ask to hear it

NEPHEW/NIECE
Explain: You asked to hear it and the price is £60

ASSISTANT
Offer something cheaper

NEPHEW/NIECE
Report what the assistant said. Tell her the quality depends on price

AUNT
Tell your nephew you didn't hear a word

. . . now continue the role play

Vocabulary practice

a alien   b complete   c immigration   d identity card

Further practice

Set students the following exercise, which can be done as written or oral work.
 Make the following passage into a dialogue between the boarding-house keeper, Paul and a member of the audience.

The boarding-house keeper told Paul and his wife that they were holding a concert for guests on Thursday evening and that Paul was to play. Paul explained that he was not really a performer and that it was out of the question. The proprietor said that that made no difference, and that he was to play all the same.

After the concert a member of the audience asked politely if he might possibly borrow the guitar. Paul replied that he could, by all means.

Begin like this
Boarding-house keeper: We are holding a concert . . .

Unit 3

Listening

Answer key
1. When he moved into his new flat
2. It made no mess and only needed feeding every two months.
3. That they are disgusting and slimy
4. Boa constrictor
5. Until he finally had to bring them face to face with the snake
6. It restricted it.
7. It did not want to eat even the best-quality dead meat.
8. The snake would only eat live food.
9. He bought kittens from local people because pet shops refused to sell him live animals as food.
10. It made him 'emotional' – he didn't like doing it.

Reading

Note on the text: RSPCA = Royal Society for the Prevention of Cruelty to Animals.

Answer key
1 staggered (l.19)   2 bizarre (l.6)   3 placid (l.28)
4 making every effort (l.34)   5 housed (l.49)   6 tame (l.56)
7 fractured (l.60)   8 worried about (l.70)

GRAMMAR GUIDE

Past simple of irregular verbs

Answer key
bred fed found fought thought went dug took flung understood strode

Past continuous

Possible answers:
While I was studying for exams, they were watching a horror film.
While we we trying to get through the traffic jam, she was calling the police.
While/when you were waiting outside the cinema, we were trying to get through the traffic jam/he was cleaning the car.

Unit 3 Teachers Notes 11

Note: *Just as* is not normally used to link two or more activities in the Past Continuous; we tend to use it when one past continuous activity is linked with a past simple action which happened at a specific point in time, eg
Just as I was dialling the number of the local police station, she walked through the door.

Past simple/past continuous

When Richard arrived she was already in the kitchen making tea.
She didn't start making tea until after Richard had arrived.

Past habits

Answer key
got worked was would leave walk would be would eat was

Vocabulary practice

Animal sets: mammals
dog, cat, rabbit, tiger, kitten – (non-rodents)
goose, budgerigar, duck – birds
rat, mouse, gerbil – rodents
salamander, snake, terrapin, alligator, boa constrictor – cold-blooded animals

Unit 4

Listening 1

1 . . . organised and led a worldwide series of expeditions.
2 . . . Operation Drake.*
3 . . . opportunities for young people to work together on projects of high adventure.
4 . . . 17 and 24.
5 . . . setting up another project on a much greater scale.
6 . . . forty expeditions . . . for a period of four years.
7 . . . fifty countries.
8 . . . carry out his tasks in difficult conditions to the best of his ability.

*Note: Sir Francis Drake (1540?–1596). Pirate and explorer who made a round-the-world voyage in 1577. He fought against the Spanish Armada in 1588.

Reading
Vocabulary practice
Answer key

a drew to a close
b look back on
c helped with
d rewarding
e erected
f in one way or another
g dollar-spinner
h memorable
i spotted
j rampaged
k magnet
l faced with
m reckons
n bivvies*
o judge

*Note: bivvies – a colloquial shortened form of 'bivouacs'

Additional practice

1 Set students the following gap-fill exercise.
Fill in the missing words to complete the text. One word only is needed for each space.
SIR WALTER RALEIGH*
Four centuries _____, in 1584, Sir Walter Raleigh's colonists founded an English-speaking settlement _____ America. Raleigh's name has always _____ linked with adventure. He was a great favourite _____ Queen Elizabeth I and was an explorer, courtier and scientist. It was _____ who introduced the potato to England, imported tobacco and _____ smoking popular.
   Raleigh _____ from Devon where his father owned several ships. Sir Walter designed and built _____ which were intended for long and

dangerous voyages. He opened ____ the New World to settlers from Europe, collected thousands of plant specimens and was the ____ of a book, 'The History of the World'.

Answer key
ago in been of he/Raleigh made came some/several up author

*****Note**: Sir Walter Raleigh was an English explorer, courtier, writer and poet who led several expeditions to North and South America during the reign of Queen Elizabeth I. Legend has it that he spread his cloak over a puddle to enable the Queen to cross with dry shoes.

2 This exercise can be done orally to check comprehension of the reading text. Read the questions out to the students.
Are the following statements true or false?
a Most participants have not benefited greatly from the experience.
b People in general are very interested in the project.
c More work has taken place than was at first anticipated.
d Operation Raleigh has a strong educational aim.
e The Venturers have all learned something new about themselves.
f The diet was often monotonous.
g Very few of the skills learned on the project will be of any use to the Venturers when they go home again.

Answer key
a False   b True   c True   d True   e True
f True   g False

GRAMMAR GUIDE

Present Perfect

For/since

Answer key

1

for	since
five minutes	Christmas
six years	last week
half a century	your birthday
some time	he left school
a fortnight	last August

2 a Anna has been waiting at the bus stop since 6.30 am.
  b Grandmother has been staying with us since Christmas Eve.
  c He has been playing tennis regularly for thirty-nine years.
  d She has been writing a novel since 19___.
  e My parents have been living in Australia for ____ years.

Just/still/yet

1 They have been studying English/French for six months.
2 She has been writing the/a book since 1982.
3 We have been decorating the house every weekend but we haven't finished yet.
4 He still hasn't sat the exam/ He hasn't sat the exam yet.
5 He has tried a few times but still has not passed his driving test.

Vocabulary practice

Answer key
1 adventure
2 judge
3 estimate
4 expeditions
5 survival
6 resourcefulness
7 camp
8 bivouacs/huts
9 cope
10 rope

Unit 5

Listening

Answer key
1 To get information about the agency
2 To help people make contact with others with similar interests
3 There are too many members and people joining.
4 To exclude undesirables
5 £75.00 a year
6 Six names, addresses and phone numbers
7 35000
8 All kinds, including politicians, actresses and dustmen
9 Fill in a questionnaire

Reading

Vocabulary check

Answer key
1 heart went out to, drawn to
2 cell, compound, Death Row, gas chamber
3 commuted
4 the straight and narrow
5 a person who has lived dangerously

Check your understanding

Answer key
1 Virginia flew out with a TV camera crew.
2 She hopes Hasan will be released in a year; she believes he killed only in self-defence. The prison authorities share neither view.
3 'He looked upon her writing as a gift from God.'

Group work

Once the listening and reading materials have been completed, the following points for discussion can be presented on a sheet to small groups of students.
1 Do you believe in love at first sight, especially if this first sight is on TV?
2 Could you do as Virginia did and fall in love with a criminal?

Intensive English

3 Can love overcome all obstacles?
4 Is it a good idea to believe that one can change one's partner in some way after marriage?
5 What is wrong with appearing as a do-gooder?
6 Do you think that 'communicating very well' is a good basis for marriage? Do you think that Virginia and Hasan really communicated very well?
7 Do you think the presence of a TV company from England could have influenced the course of the story in any way?
8 Is the prison officer being unduly cynical about the motives of women who marry prisoners? And about the motives of prisoners who marry in prison?
9 Is it enough for Virginia to do what her eldest son says and not care what anyone else thinks?
10 What might other people think?

Writing

Present these instructions to the class:
Look at the reading text again. Check each paragraph and make a note of the main point or points.
When you have done this, using only your notes, write a short summary of the passage in not more than 200 words.

GRAMMAR GUIDE

Past perfect

Answer key
1 realised, had forgotten, had shut
2 stole, had bought
3 arrived, had burned
4 had got, felt
5 had tasted, knew, was
6 had just begun, burst
7 started, had arrived/arrived
8 crashed, had had
9 found out, had planned, appeared or found out, planned, had appeared
10 had left, realised, had left

Unit 5 Teachers Notes 17

Vocabulary practice

These are not meant to be rigid distinctions. There is a room for argument.

GOOD	BAD
competent	cautious
outgoing	unimaginative
creative	plodding
calm	mean
silent	placid
irrepressible	talkative
careful	serious
cheerful	
vivacious	

Unit 6

Listening

Lisa: Motives – children and financial security. (This is not stated in so many words in the text but can be deduced from the whole statement.)
Frances: Motives – Charles was persistent about getting married. He was different, had charisma and finally broke down her resistance.

Reading
Check your understanding
A   Order of occurrence: 6,4,1,8,2,5,7,3
B   1 True   2 False   3 True   4 True   5 False
    6 False 7 False   8 True

GRAMMAR GUIDE

Adjectives + word order

Answer key
1 a luxurious white leather armchair
2 an involved (and) spine-chilling ghost story
3 a handsome, sensitive boy
4 a sprawling, characterless modern city
5 the latest depressing news/depressing latest news (alternative answer when 'latest news' is a set phrase as used in broadcasting)
6 a cool, clear, shallow stream
7 a pale, weak (and) sickly baby
8 a stylish blue silk dress
9 a rusty old secondhand car

By + until

Answer key
1 until   3 until   5 by   7 until
2 by   4 by   6 until 8 by

Vocabulary practice

Answer key
1 bride   5 prospective   9   marry
2 couples   6 best man   10 engagement
3 marriages   7 wedding
4 get married   8 bridal

Unit 7

Listening

Mrs Masters' statement
Husband doesn't think a wife should work.
She helped pay for his studies for two years.
They used to go dancing but then they stopped.
He became obsessive.
He stopped looking after himself.
He lost interest in having a social life.
He paid no attention to her.
He lives in a world of his own.
He's shorter than she is.
He neglects personal hygiene.
He doesn't wash his feet.
He chews his fingernails.
His smell and appearance appal her.
They didn't talk much.
He only eats potato chips and biscuits.
He spent one year doing odd jobs.
He sits all day in front of a screen.
She's glad they have no children.
He shrugs his shoulders at talk of having a divorce and says nothing.

Mr Master's statement
She gave up work after he finished university.
A job would do her good.
He would like her to meet people.
She's too tired to go dancing.
They don't like the same things.
She has an obsession about cleanliness
She cleans an already spotless house.
She washes his nearly-clean socks.
She has lost her personality.
She is boring and bored.
She criticises his appearance.
She usually gives a twisted version of events.
She nags at him for working.
She doesn't cook.
He has to look after himself.
She keeps interrupting him while he's working.
He has to work, he works from home.
She doesn't appreciate what he does.
He wanted children, she didn't.

Having a child would improve his wife's outlook.
He doesn't want a divorce but thinks things must change.

Group work

Prepare work sheets for a group discussion, using as many of these points as you feel necessary:
- Is the Marriage Guidance counselling service a good thing?
- Do you think this marriage guidance counsellor performed a useful service?
- Look at the following list of reasons which could be given as grounds for divorce. Place them in order of importance:

Lack of personal hygiene
Ugliness
Partner is growing old.
Partner is overweight.
Partner goes out every night.
Partner invites very boring people to dinner regularly.
Partner spends all free time repairing the car.
Partner never remembers your birthday.
Partner spends every evening watching television.
Partner is a compulsive complainer.
Partner deliberately brings home loads of unsuitable things from the supermarket so that you are forced to do the shopping yourself.
Partner persistently uses the bathroom as a reading room.
Partner never has anything new to say.

- What do you feel are the worst possible grounds for divorce, and are they included in the list above?

Reading

Check your understanding

Answer key
Where – Alaska
    Gallatin, Tennessee
    Hal's father
Why – Hal said his wife was cruel and inhuman; Wendy said that he behaved like a 10-year-old.
    State law prevents him from taking a job because of his age.
What – Cruel and inhuman treatment was given as grounds for a divorce.
    $30 a week
    The child was to remain with the mother. Hal had annual visitation rights.
A 'Catch-22' is a situation from which there is no escape (taken from the title of the novel by Joseph Heller).

GRAMMAR GUIDE

Must + have to

Answer key
1. must
2. have to
3. mustn't
4. have to
5. had to
6. mustn't
7. have to
8. must
9. mustn't
10. have to

Needn't/don't have to/ don't need to

Answer key
a We don't have to
b He didn't have to
c You don't have to/You needn't *
d I wouldn't have to
e I needn't

*__Note__: Choice depends on the speaker's intention – is the speaker being authoritative or commenting on a habitual action which irritates?

Phrasal verbs

Answer key

1.
   a get up
   b get on
   c get down
   d get out

2.
   a go on
   b go over
   c go out
   d go on

3.
   a give up
   b set up
   c write up
   d end up

Mixed phrasal verbs

Answer key
1. talk over
2. find out
3. put down
4. look after
5. pick at
6. Come along

Unit 8

Reading

Notes on text:
junk food: food that is easy to prepare, has minimal nutritional value, often full of chemical additives
larder: originally a cold room off the kitchen, used for storing food
purloin: a humorous word meaning 'steal'
green shimmer: going mouldy
sleuthing: detective work

Listening

Answer key
a Because he then started piano lessons as well
b Two – piano and horn (three if you count 'keyboards')
c They all had lessons on different days.
d The school was three miles away, the horn was heavy and the bus service was unreliable.
e To leap in the air and kick each other in the face
f Yes, most of the time!

Further practice

Set the following additional exercise on the listening material. Put it on to a worksheet.

Arrange the events below in the order in which they happened:
a Simon's daughter started music lessons.
b The oldest son became a member of a rock group.
c Simon's son joined a chamber orchestra as a horn player.
d The eldest child started school.
e The younger son joined a wind band.
f The boys took up karate.
g The second son began piano lessons.
h His daughter joined the Brownies.

Answer key
1 d   2 g   3 a   4 e   5 h   6 f   7 c   8 b

GRAMMAR GUIDE

Should/ought to had/better

Answer key
2 a We had better hurry up.
   b We had better report it to the police.
   c We ought to buy a good camera.
   d She should be more sensible.
   e He should/ought to give up driving.
   f He ought to get a new job.
   g We ought to buy a vineyard.
   h They should have carried an umbrella.
   i I had better take them back to the shop.
   j She should/ought to get more sleep.

Phrasal verbs practice

Answer key
go on   give up   wolf down   throw up   come down   breaks down
let up   take up

Vocabulary practice

Answer key
1 unimportant   invalid   improvident
   uncommon   unsympathetic   inaccessible
   uncleanliness   impersonal   unnecessary
   uneasy   unsuitable   undemonstratively
   unoriginal   inexpensive   unfortunately
2 a uneasy
   b uncommon
   c inaccessible
   d improvident
   e unoriginal

Unit 9

Listening

Answer key

Profile of a Career

Bert: BBC Sound Engineer
Secondary Education: *Grammar* School
Qualifications: 5 O'levels including *Maths* and *English*

First Employer: *College of Science*
Annual Salary: £ *156*
Training: *Day release* and evening classes.
Further Qualifications obtained: Physics A'level (failed *the rest*)
Length of service: Five years

Second Employer: *Air Force*
Training: RAF Trade course
Qualification: *Ground Wireless Mechanic*
Position obtained: *Control Room* operator
Length of service: *2 years*

Third Employer: *College*

Fourth Employer: British Broadcasting Corporation
Name of job: *Technical Assistant*
Training: *Two Years* in-house training
Title after training: Sound engineer
Department: Recording Unit

Fifth employer: *East African* Broadcasting Corporation (on secondment from British Broadcasting Corporation)
Further qualifications: Practical experience in *Outside Broadcasting*
Purpose: Technical assistance in expanding broadcasting service

Sixth employer: BBC, Training Department then BBC Television Outside Broadcasts.
Length of service: About 1 Year

Seventh employer: BBC, Outside Broadcasts

Check your understanding
Answer key
1 a False   b True   c True   d False   e True
   f True
2 apprenticeship: a period spent learning a trade or craft
   probationary basis: trial period
   messed about with: used but not in any serious way
   broadened the horizons: discovered new possibilities
   manning control rooms: working as an operator in control rooms
   secondment: a temporary transfer to another company or institution
   fundamental knowledge: basic understanding (used here by the speaker to mean in contrast with practical experience)
   pageantry: ceremonial splendour
   turned on by: excited by
3 BBC: British Broadcasting Corporation
   OB: Outside Broadcasts
   RAF: Royal Air Force
   TV: Television

Notes on listening passage
O-Level: Ordinary Level of the General Certificate of Education (GCE), normally taken by 16-year-olds at school
A-Level: Advanced Level of the GCE examination, taken by 18-year-olds

Reading

Answer key
College of Science
Royal Air Force
a BBC
b College of Science
c BBC
d College of Science
e RAF
f East African Broadcasting Corporation
g BBC Outside Broadcasts
h BBC Outside Broadcasts

Word order

Answer key
1. (His) birth was registered in Hounslow in 1986.
2. Take (it) to the airport immediately.
3. (He) went to night classes in Leeds every evening after work.
4. He came back with his family to the hotel at 2 am.
5. They had been living quietly in East Africa for two years.
6. Look carefully at the advertisement.
7. They came up to town a few months later.
8. (He) worked on happily in that country for six more months.
9. We want to invite them to the country next year.
10. He was fortunately not caught up in the fighting.

Vocabulary practice

Answer key
1 After age minimum become gained classes up went back further since more for for many visit
2 civil servant mechanic engineer technician operator

Unit 10

Reading

Correct order of the three parts of the text: B C A

Word definitions
Part A:
engages the services of: employs (often on a temporary or ad hoc basis)
PAYE (Pay As You Earn): a system of taxation whereby income tax is deducted at source by the employer from the employee's salary
tax allowances: concessions which allow the offsetting of certain categories of expenditure, or financial loss against tax
in the long term: in the (distant) future
venture: risky undertaking
cottage industry: a business carried on from one's own home
make a dent in: make an impression on, reduce

Part B:
streaming: pouring, flooding through
bread riots: popular uprisings in protest against food shortages
woefully: sadly, regrettably
moonlighter: someone who works casually, for cash, and pays no income tax
(politicians) of all hues: of all political parties
at a stretch: without a break
black economy: unofficial economy involving cash payments not reported for tax purposes
plumbing: installation and repair of water/gas pipes

Part C:
compensate: make up for
on her books: on her register of employees
overdraft facility: an arrangement with a bank to draw money beyond one's credit
spurred: stimulated
National Insurance: compulsory payments deduced from salary to provide for health care, old age pensions etc.

Check your understanding
Answer key
1   30%
2   They work 'illegally', ie they do not register as self-employed but remain on the unemployment register. They usually take jobs

requiring no special skills and are casually employed and paid in cash.
3   25 cleaners
4   There was a shortage of good domestic cleaners and no agency to recruit them.
5   One job created by employers to two jobs created by the self-employed

Group discussion

Make worksheets with all, or a selection of, the following questions and give to small groups for discussion:
Discuss these points, take notes and compare your findings with those of other groups.
Look at the list of businesses below and decide whether you think they are manufacturing industries or not.

Shipbuilding	Knife sharpening
Garage	Chemist's shop
Insurance company	Pottery
Textiles	British Rail
Computer importer	Computer software house
Coalmining	Landscape gardening
Farming	Horse breeding
Garden centre	Window cleaning
Temporary secretarial agency	The Welsh National Opera

- Would you rather work in a 'service industry', like insurance or the hotel business, or in 'manufacturing'?
- Do you think it is wrong for people to do work for cash without telling the authorities and without paying income tax?
- Would you get excited about running a cleaning agency?
- What questions would you ask a prospective cleaner in an interview?
- Do you think putting leaflets through a door is a good method of advertising?
- If you started your own business, what would you like to do?
- If you started your own business, how much money would you expect to be earning after the first eight months?
- Would you be able to work on your own or with one or two others, or do you need very many other people around you at work?
- Is it a good idea to take out an overdraft when you are starting a business, or would your prefer to provide the initial capital entirely out of your savings?

GRAMMAR GUIDE

Answer key
1   The new typist who came to work here last week is very good.
2   Lake Windermere, which is only ten miles long, is probably the longest lake in England.

Unit 10 Teachers Notes 29

3 The horse which I picked out won the race.
4 Where are the shoes that I wore (which I was wearing) this morning?
5 Jim, whose wife is very ill, can't come to the match.
6 The yellow car which belongs to Brian has been badly damaged.
7 Janet Watson, whom you saw at the last meeting, is over there.
8 The dish that (which) you have just eaten contained pieces of snake.
9 Mr Bishop, whose house is for sale, was on the phone.

Vocabulary practice

Answer key
1 plumber: installs and mends water and gas pipes
  totter: searches through rubbish tips for saleable items
  nightwatchman: guards public buildings and factories at night
  caretaker: organises the cleaning of housing blocks or public buildings
  ostler: looks after horses
  night porter: acts as hotel receptionist at night
  midwife: helps mothers at childbirth
  bookmaker: takes gamblers' bets on horses and dogs
  impresario: arranges concerts and entertainments
  insurance broker: acts as middleman between clients and insurance companies

3 a cash flow   f bankrupt
  b savings   g investments
  c long term   h accountant
  d overdraft   i house
  e business plan   j repayments

Pronunciation

Answer key

early	feature	bread	break	create
years	reason	dead	steak	
earnings	leaflet	breakfast		
heard	teach	ready		
	cleaning			
	appear			
	stream			
	teapot			

Unit 11

Reading

Check your understanding
Answer key
1.
lot	situation
consolidating	strengthening
bayonet	sharp blade
gross	unacceptable
injustices	discrepancies
industriousness	hard work
fend for	look after
focused attention on	highlighted
studiously ignored	deliberately disregarded
tabloid press	popular newspapers

2. a Women will still make an effort to look feminine even while they are taking on a traditionally aggressive male role.
   b Little or none
   c To review the achievements or otherwise of women over the past ten years
   d Women may now be deployed as front-line troops, instead of playing a supporting role at a safe distance, as in past conflicts
   e If education cannot be afforded for all the children in a family, boys take priority because they are traditionally regarded as superior.

Listening

Answer key
1. ... her children were very small and her mother was available to help her. She also needed extra money desperately.
2. ... making one sample blouse.
3. ... fixing a ruffle/ binding the neck/ attaching sleeves/ putting in darts/ sewing the side seams.
4. ... twelve-and-a-half pence each; the current rate is £1 per hour.
5. ... the children were all at home during the day. There was no separate room to work in. She didn't want to endanger the children by leaving needles and pins lying around.

GRAMMAR GUIDE

Word building I

Answer key
dejected rejected form entrain trained emerged retrained merged submerged fend defend performed invested divesting

Word order

Answer key
The tabloid press has studiously ignored the Women's Movement over the years.
In any case, I was only able to work at night after the children were in bed.
Everywhere thousands of women are being exploited daily as cheap labour.
Women who have been trained to kill will be wearing nail polish and lipstick when they do it.

Word building II

Answer key
1 equality
2 politics
3 economy
4 legality
5 explicitness
6 similarity
7 development
8 society

Making sense

Answer key
1 make
2 the type of worker
3 brought out
4 manufactured
5 had all day to work

Unit 12

Reading

Before looking at their part of the text, students should use a dictionary to find the meanings of these key words:

Part A
Vocabulary check: Find out what these mean . . .

a two-tier system	pursuit
artisans	motivation
gossip	former

Part B
Vocabulary check: Find out what these mean . . .

run deeply	generate
to a large extent	to drop
determine	synonymous
to engineer	
substantially	
sums (of money)	

Part C
Vocabulary check: find out what these mean . . .

current	to be likely to (do something)
span	prevailed
to the fore	exploded
alike	sensibility

Check your understanding
Answer key
Part A
1 Merchants worked for profits, artisans for wages.
2 It has become a basic human need.
3 Work and leisure went together.
4 The upper classes felt that work was demeaning and expected others to work for them.

Unit 12 Teachers Notes

Part B
1 By making it possible for mechanical, repetitive jobs to be done by machines rather than people
2 The computer and leisure industries
3 The people who have money and those who don't

Part C
1 The working week will be reduced, paid holidays will be increased
2 Sixty hours
3 A new resurgence of working practices
4 Because most governments have been slow to recognise and provide for the problems posed by increased leisure

Additional material

Group work

Give these instructions to the class:
Working in your groups, appoint a spokesperson to tell the class briefly what your section of text is about. Listen to all three summaries, making notes as you listen.
Prepare a worksheet with these questions (students to answer them *without* referring to the text):
Are these statements true or false?
1 There is no reason to work other than to provide for your personal needs.
2 It is certain that engineering technology could generate a period of growth and prosperity.
3 Before the Industrial Revolution, people's attitudes to work were different from those of today.
4 People have always wanted to work.
5 Governments are not taking the future needs of non-working people very seriously.
6 Priority should be given to improving life on a social level.
7 A lot of workers who dislike their jobs feel useless.
8 New technology is replacing natural resources.
9 New technology means new jobs in several fields.
10 The provision of extended opportunities for education could play a valuable part in our future well-being.

Answer key
1 False   5 True   9 True
2 False   6 True   10 True
3 True   7 True
4 False   8 True

GRAMMAR GUIDE

Prepositional verbs

Answer key

1	look for	6	look round
2	divide . . . into	7	go up
3	distinguish between	8	taking on
4	pay . . . into	9	arrive at
5	pouring . . . into	10	applied for

Past irregular verbs

Answer key
clung swung found wound bound hung slid lit came
held flung stuck shot

Unit 13

Opening activity

Label the parts of the bicycle correctly from the list below:
brake	brake lever
chain	crossbar
frame	gearwheels
hub	lamp
mudguard	pannier
pedal	saddle
spoke	tyre
wheel	

Listening

Before listening, check the meaning of these words:
shed	to turn out
élitist	limelight
outstrip	eerie silence
podgy	bit of a giggle
egg someone on	to give way to
ignominy	

36 Intensive English

Answer key
1. Very popular. Most cities around the world have their own marathon event each year.
2. Royal Processions and the Boat Race.
3. Perhaps cycling is regarded as an elitist sport?
4. Because it is very early in the morning. Most people are still asleep!
5. Podgy middle-aged executives/ lean and mean youngsters/ joke cyclists
6. Village people feed them and encourage them.
7. It is the last long steep hill after fifty miles of cycling.
8. Tight, long shorts and close-fitting satiny shirts plus a cap worn back to front.

Note: The Boat Race between Oxford and Cambridge universities, which takes place on the River Thames. Each side has a team of oarsmen who row from Putney to Mortlake.
to egg someone on = to encourage.

Reading

Answer key
a) | Matching Headlines
1. 'Team Disqualified'
2. 'Devon Man all washed up'
3. 'WPC Hit by Runaway Granny'
4. 'Trams Sabotage Cyclists'
5. 'Seventh Man on a Bike'
6. 'Veterans Protest Race'
7. 'Brighton Run Latest'

b) Check your understanding:
1. They were riding a horse, not a bicycle.
2. Not at all experienced, he was a beginner.
3. A women's social and charitable organisation associated with the Church of England
4. Backwards
5. None – they were all wearing safety belts.

c) Meanings:
careered: run wildly and out of control
knocks it out of you: exhausts you
drift in: come in slowly, a few at a time
beyond repair: cannot be repaired
theorise: attempt an explanation
ugly scenes: violent confrontation
reinstatement: readmittance to the race
adamant: obstinate and unbending in an opinion
pile into an obstruction: crash into an obstacle and form a heap

GRAMMAR GUIDE

Expressing preferences

Answer key
2 Would you like a lift home? No, I'd prefer to walk.
   Would you like to eat out? No, I'd prefer to stay at home.
   Would you like to see the/a film? No, I'd prefer to go another/some other time.
   Do you want to drive to Scotland? No, I'd prefer to travel by train.
   Do you want to go camping? No, I'd prefer to stay in a hotel.
3 Shall I buy a motorbike? No, I'd prefer to spend the money on a washing machine rather than buy a bike.
   Shall we take a trip to the coast? No, I'd prefer to go walking in the country rather than take a trip to the coast.
   Shall we spend an evening with Joe and Ellen? No, I'd prefer to stay at home rather than . . .
   Shall we get tickets for a musical? No, I'd prefer to see a serious play rather than . . .
   Shall I take your sister out for dinner? No, she'd prefer to eat at home rather than . . .
4 Would you prefer to/rather drink red or white wine?
   Would you rather see a tennis or a football match?
   Would you rather stay (here) longer or go home?
   Would you rather play squash or tennis?
   Would you rather learn Russian or Spanish?
   Would you rather travel by air or by car?

Irregular verbs practice

Answer key

swung	read
sped	got
led	strung
took	took
fell	wrung
bled	shone
	won

Gap test

Answer key

cross	rest
take	keep
travel	into
turn	up
straight	mad
chance	past
before	along
by	fork
top	just

Writing

The following additional exercise may be set to students in pairs:
Role Play + Writing
Student 1 is a news reporter. You are to interview a competitor who has just come last in a race with 75 entrants. You know several things went wrong.
Find out if the competitor would have liked anything to be different.
Take notes and write an article for the sports section of the local newspaper.
Student 2 is the competitor who came in last. Decide what kind of race you took part in. Several things went wrong. Talk to the reporter and explain what you'd prefer to be different next time.
Write a report on the race from *your* viewpoint for the committee of your sports club.

Unit 14

Listening

Answer key
1. Ancient Egyptian times
2. They adopted the game from the Greeks.
3. Fertility rites
4. The villagers played football instead of practising military skills.
5. Hundred of people play up and down the length of a village.

Group task
In the group, the findings of the survey should be collated and a report made to the other groups in the class. Students could also construct a bar graph and take notes as they listen to the other reports. Write down the points they have in common and any surprising differences, so that a complete picture can be assembled.

Reading

Before reading, check the meaning of these words. Use a dictionary.

to herald	an ally	to taunt
flashy (car)	to turn out	a few bob
armour-clad	good-natured	the pitch
to cram	the norm	unruly
thug	to combat	spectator

Answer key
Correct order: D B A C

GRAMMAR GUIDE

Conditional I

Answer key
a issue/will become safer
b clean/ will take
c don't sell/ won't get
d make/ will be
e throw/ will breathe
f beat/ will be
g refuse/ will be

Intensive English

Vocabulary

Answer key

shoot	football
punch	boxing
throw	wrestling
strike	baseball
bowl	cricket
pass	rugby
serve	tennis
pot	snooker
drive	golf
jump	parachuting
stem	skiing
cast	fishing
tack	sailing
crawl	swimming
abseil	climbing

Unit 15

Listening

Check the meaning

suburb: an outer area of a town where people live
to depict: to represent with a picture or to describe in words
desolate: sad and deserted
flyover: a bridge carrying one road over the top of another
maze: a puzzle for which there is no obvious way out and many misleading paths
to spot: to notice
take one's bearings: make a mental note of one's position
precinct: an enclosed area (in this case containing only shops)
ample: enough, a generous amount
to bound: to run, taking very long strides

Answer key
1 a note, spotting, took my bearings, look back, saw, look down
   b drove up, to descend, go down, climbed up, abseiling, bound up, pull down
   c strange (city), unfamiliar, the maze
   d skyscraper, shopping precincts, flyovers, underpasses, underground and overhead walkways, urban motorway, stairways, platforms, subway
2 a . . . to avoid a lot of problems.
   b . . . an arena where bullfighting took place.
   c . . . shopping precincts, a market, a bus station, several car parks and a maze of stairways, walkways and subways.
   d . . . he might not be able to get back to the car park before it closed.
3 Local people were not able to help because they were not familiar with the way through the complex.

Pair work

1 Subway   2 Shopping precinct   3 Car park
4 Skyscraper   5 Urban motorway

Reading

Check the meaning

frayed: loose threads along the cut or torn edge of a piece of material
casual: informal
poseur (*slang*): person who behaves strangely to produce an effect

gear (*slang*): clothes, normally fashionable ones
bleach: liquid chemical which removes colour
discerning: having good taste, discriminating
horn-rimmed: spectacle frames made of animal horn
stretch to: manage or succeed
painstakingly: with great care
lanky: tall and thin
slash: cut with a sharp blade
gratify: give pleasure or satisfaction
to sport: to wear
tails: a formal evening coat with a long shaped back divided into two from the waist downwards
darned: fabric repaired by weaving wool with a sewing needle
patched: fabric repaired by sewing a piece of material over the damaged area

Check your understanding

Answer key
1 bleach – to remove some colour from the fabric
   razors – for slashing or cutting new clothes
   paperclips – to wear as earrings
2 They were bleached, slashed, frayed and quickly worn into holes.
3 (b)
4 His spectacles are now horn-rimmed, he has very short hair. His shirts and jacket are formal, worn with a black tie or no tie at all. His jeans are patched with contrasting material.
5 The contrast between what is worn above and below the waist
6 A collar which is high, stiff and has the points pressed out to resemble wings.

GRAMMAR GUIDE

Sentence transformation

Animals can show more aggression if they are provoked.
We should not congratulate ourselves.
The viewing public alleges that reports on TV are biased.
My friends and I held a celebration at the pub.
It is one of the few studies that confidently connects TV and violence.
The authorities ought to place a ban on such films.
Cave Art originates from the superstitions of ancient tribes.

Vocabulary

Answer key

Tomorrow	mine-clearing	Poles/Canadians
Yesterday	land	parachutes
birthday	beaches	boats
Ditchling	France	airfields
ten miles	weather	wooden gliders
due south	Canadians/Poles	airsick

Unit 16

Opening discussion

Answer key
Boris Becker – German tennis player, Men's Singles Champion at Wimbledon in 1986
Muhammed Ali – former American world heavyweight boxing champion
Pele – Brazilian soccer champion
Daley Thomson – British athlete, Gold Medallist in the Olympic Pentathlon
Zola Budd – South African athlete; acquired British citizenship in order to compete in world competitions

Reading

Check your understanding

Answer key
1 The Coliseum
2 A slip of a girl in a green vest (Nawal el Moutawakel)
3 The significance of the occasion
4 The Coliseum
5 Abebe Bikila
6 The whole of Africa
7 The world
8 The whole continent of Africa
9 Nawal el Moutawakel's success
10 Morocco

Listening

Check the meaning

thud: a dull sound
fixation: obsession
allay: reduce
ostentatious: obvious
serialise: to publish or broadcast in instalments
incredulous: disbelieving
counterpart: opposite number, equivalent
overburden: overload
public school: in Britain, an exclusive, fee-paying independent school
resurrect: revive, bring back into existence
discomfiture: embarrassment, humiliation

Intensive English

Answer key
1. C
2. False
3. The adventures of rich and privileged young men
4. In terms of underprivileged and poor athletes triumphing against all the odds
5. The search for a white athlete or boxer capable of challenging the dominance of the black champions
6. A white world heavyweight boxing champion
7. Because comic papers appeared to equate the dominance of blacks in world sport with a threat to the stability of the then British Empire.
8. Because they wished to believe that white athletes were superior.
9. Boxing and athletics were dominated by blacks.
10. He won 5 gold medals at the 1936 Olympics in Berlin, and Hitler left the stadium rather than watch the medals being presented.
11. Eighty years
12. As an affirmation of national identity and pride

GRAMMAR GUIDE

Passive infinitive

Answer key
1. to be forgotten
   to be given
   to be forgiven
   to be loved
   to be opened
   to be ordered
   to be removed
   to be taken
   to be used
   to be won
2. Not to be opened until Christmas Day
   Lots of prizes to be won
   To be opened only in case of emergency
   Not to be forgotten!
   To be ordered at least one day in advance

Passive – Present simple

Answer key (sample responses)
1. Sport is played by many people.
2. Tennis is watched by a lot of people
3. Sports personalities are very much admired.
4. Local competitions are not organised by anyone.
5. Sport is broadcast a lot on the radio.
6. Cricket is not well known.
7. . . . is played most by . . .

8   Most sport is shown on TV on . . .
9   . . . is treated . . . by the newspaper.
10 . . . is/is not well attended.

Passive – Past simple

Answer key
1   No, he wasn't. He was assassinated in Dallas.
2   No, they weren't. They were written by Ian Fleming.
3   No, it wasn't. It was invented by the Americans.
4   No, it wasn't. It was first conquered by a New Zealander and a Nepalese Sherpa.
5   No, they weren't. They were made in the UK.
6   No, they weren't. The British Isles were last successfully invaded in 1066.
7   No, it wasn't. It was composed by Beethoven.
8   No, it wasn't. It was dropped on Hiroshima.
9   No, they weren't. They were originally held in ancient Greece.
10 No, they weren't. They were played at 78 rpm.

Vocabulary practice

exclaim   demand   announce
marathon   400 m hurdles   800 m   3000 m
highest   incomparable
years   1984   1960   1965   1983
successes   status   feat   conquest

Unit 18

Reading

Check the meaning
culinary: concerned with cooking
substitute: alternative
palate: a discriminating sense of taste
textured vegetable protein: a meat substitute made from soya
herds: large groups (of animals)
ball bearings: small steel balls used to make machinery run smoothly
canapé: a small savoury appetiser
gourmet market: discriminating customers
look-alike: substitute
revolting: disgusting
trail of slime: silver, shiny trail left on the ground by snails
the last word: the most fashionable
fad: a temporary liking for something fashionable
phased out: gradually discontinued
flash in the pan: a short-lived phenomenon

Answer key
1. Meatballs and caviar
2. Sturgeon and salmon
3. Because the sturgeon is being destroyed by the increasing pollution of its habitat and by over-fishing.
4. Sturgeon caviar = black eggs, snail caviar = large white eggs
5. Tibet
6. 6000 francs
7. People have resistance to eating the eggs of a creature that leaves a trail of slime.
8. It is a polite way of saying that he found Moscow restaurants mediocre.
9. They resemble small oily black balls, as in a machine.
10. Snail farming is becoming popular.

Listening

Answer key
1. Because of public pressure against the use of additives
2. It makes additive-free food.
3. 700 tonnes
4. Customer demand
5. Bright yellow

Writing

An additional assignment to give for homework, perhaps:
A friend from another country has asked you to send a recipe for your favourite national dish. Write a letter giving a list of ingredients and careful cooking instructions.
Remember to set out your letter correctly!

Project

(Prepare a short worksheet.)
Working in small groups, plan a menu for a very special dinner to be given to celebrate an important event.
The dinner should consist of several courses or dishes which can be from one country or several countries.
You might also like to design table decorations and the menu card.
Present this to the other groups, giving reasons for your choices.
Take a vote on the plan which is likely to be the most successful.

GRAMMAR GUIDE

Present simple commentary

Answer key
places	hurls
waits	pushes
passes	moves
dribbles	doesn't
flips	swerves
smashes	lets
gathers	

Vocabulary practice

Answer key
budget	coat hangers
the washing	creases
washing-up	coin
the shopping	

Unit 17

Reading

Check your understanding

Answer key
1. a Correct
   b No – Anton was born in Austria.
   c No – he followed the example of a precaution taken by a chef at Maxims.
   d Correct
   e No – he stayed with them while he was looking for work.
3. College of Catering – 'Pudding school'
   gained qualifications – picked up various qualifications
   I wanted to travel – the travel bug bit me
   working hard – slogging away
   improve my language – getting my English up to scratch
   my English lacked something – my English had yawning gaps in it

Listening

Check the meaning

croupier: person who works at the gaming tables in a casino
pocket money: personal spending money
obsessive: having a fixed idea which occupies a great deal of a person's thoughts
gadget: a small item of useful equipment
an archaeological dig: an excavation searching for buried antiquities
fluffy: having a light and airy texture
genes: materials in our body chemistry which control our inherited characteristics
yolk: the yellow centre of an egg

Check your understanding

Answer key
1. (b)
   (a)
   (b)
   (c)
   (c)

6 Because of the connection between some additives and allergies and also because they don't like food being tampered with.

GRAMMAR GUIDE

Passive perfect

Practice

Answer key
1 a A substitute for caviar has recently been demanded by restaurateurs.
   b Snails have always been regarded by gourmets as a great delicacy.
   c A great deal of time has been spent by Alain Chatillon developing caviar.
   d The taste and quality of his snail caviar has been improved by Chatillon.
2 a These potatoes haven't been cooked (by you).
   b All the old furniture was thrown away (by them).
   c The clock was not repaired (by him).
   d The exhibition has been organised by the local women's group.
   e Our car was stolen by someone called Thatcher.
   f The announcement was read out by a palace spokesman.
   g My flat has been redecorated by some friends.
   h The report was read by only one person.

Prepositions

Answer key
on   across/to   in   by   to   up   about/around   at   in   on   into/as

Been + gone

Answer key
1 been
2 gone
3 been/ gone
4 been/ gone/ been
5 been/ gone

Unit 19

Reading

Check the meaning

plume: a feather-shaped cloud of smoke or radiation
predicted: foretold, prophesied
abortive: unsuccessful
accident-prone: fallible, liable to make mistakes
spill: release
manned (by): staffed
precaution: a measure taken beforehand
fanciful: over-imaginative
deplete: reduce
contaminates: pollutes
uninhabitable: incapable of being lived in
collision: head-on crash
allay fears: reassure
molten: melted
eventuality: a happening
earth's crust: the outer layer of the earth's surface

Check your understanding

Answer key
1   Oil, coal, gas etc, formed over millions of years from decaying plant life
    to reassure the public
    a mass of fluid metal and concrete where the temperature is thousands of degrees Celsius
    build a wall to contain it
2   Governments have made a special point of saying . . .
    controlling atomic power for the production of electricity etc.
    a country's productive riches, eg coal, agricultural land, forests, etc.
    mined
    an uncontrollable reaction, in the core of a nuclear reactor
    a catastrophe to the environment
3   a True   b True (according to the text)   c True
    d False   e False   f True

GRAMMAR GUIDE

Vocabulary practice

Answer key
1 aroused   4 dismissed
2 won   5 presented
3 overflowed 6 pick

Word sets

1 Neutral
  energy   research   reactor   electricity
  ecological power   scientists
2 Negative
  accident   atom   catastrophic
  melt-down   dangerous   radioactive
  contaminates   uninhabitable awakened fears
  warlike   uncontrollable
3 Positive
  safe   survival   efficient   shield
  cheap   peaceful   clean   heroic
  self-sacrifice   white coats

Unit 20

Reading

Check the meaning

spawn: give rise to, result in
hyperbole: exaggeration
candour: honesty
halo: the nimbus of light traditionally shown round the heads of saints
hailed (as): greeted, regarded (as)
steadfastly: firmly, determinedly
exuberance: energetic high spirits
ensnare: trap, make helpless

Check your understanding

Answer key
1 losing popularity
  a 7" recording disc with one popular song on each side
  penniless
  has had enough of
2 relief, aid
3 a False   b False   c True   d True   e False

Listening

Answer key
1 £72,000
2 $100 million
3 Band Aid, Live Aid, Sport Aid
4 'I thought the givers of money would eventually stop providing.'
5 The UN General Assembly debate the crisis on the continent of Africa.
6 a El Abeid
  b Khartoum
  c Greece (runners from Mount Olympus)
  d Warsaw, Poland
  e Italy
  f France
  g England
  h Dublin, Ireland
  i New York, USA
7 To fly with Geldof and the runner on Concorde to New York.
8 To make people show that they care.

GRAMMAR GUIDE

Conditional 3

Answer key
1 If they hadn't taken an early holiday on the south coast they wouldn't have had beautiful weather.
2 If Geldof had not written a song to raise money he wouldn't have been able to help famine victims.
3 If we hadn't left home late we wouldn't have got caught up in the Bank Holiday traffic jam.
4 If she hadn't cheated in the exams and been caught, she wouldn't have been disqualified.
5 If we hadn't had dinner at our local Tandoori restaurant, we wouldn't both have felt ill the next day.
6 If I had listened to her directions on how to get to the club, I wouldn't have got hopelessly lost.

Past perfect inversion

Answer key
1 Had they known their family would be large they would not have built a house that was too small.
2 Had I known he had no driving licence, I wouldn't have lent him my car.
3 Had we not worked hard for a year, we couldn't have taken a trip round the world.
4 Had he not studied a lot he wouldn't have passed all the exams with very (such) high marks.
5 Had we realised they were so tired, we would have taken them home.
6 Had he known we were all in the waiting room, he wouldn't have left the building.

Vocabulary practice

Answer key
1 prevention
2 conscience
3 cause
4 collection
5 donations

Unit 1   Listening script

The Eco-House: An Ideal Home

Presenter: When it comes to fuel costs, the attention of the world seems to centre on the production or extraction of oil, coal or gas. Heating and hot water prices always seem to depend on the cost of fuel, and attention is rarely focused on using heating fuel in more economical ways and preventing waste. And yet this is a topic which has increasingly engaged the attention of conservationists and environmentalists throughout the world, not least in Britain. Radio World has sent its roving reporter, Julia Savage, to talk to one of the pioneers of ecological living, Lisa Strangewater, who first started building an ecologically acceptable life in the late 1960s.
Julia: Lisa, how did you come to be interested in the environment in the first place?
Lisa: Well, I have to tell you that even before my children were born we were both – my husband and I – interested in health food. I was working for a breakfast cereal company in Welwyn Garden City and I suppose it was only natural to think of making our own yoghurt out on the balcony. But since my parents came from southern Italy, I didn't really take to city life. I was very relieved when my husband inherited this piece of land in Cheshire. I was glad to get away.
Julia: Where was this exactly?
Lisa: Well, it was not too far from Knutsford, in the Pennine foothills, actually. It was a broken-down thatched cottage right in the middle of a primeval wood. It had just a couple of acres of woods round it, full of nettles. It wasn't that much to look at, but we liked it. It hadn't been lived in for twenty years, but I loved it immediately. The ground drainage was pretty bad though, and you had to wear wellies every time you went outdoors, but it was all right.
    When we first acquired it we sort of camped out on the stone-flagged floor of the living-room. We lit a fire in the open range, using logs we'd gathered in our own woods. It even had a baking oven at the side, just like a pizza oven, so I felt quite at home. Very romantic. But the sparks set the thatch on fire and since we didn't have any electricity or telephone or even piped water the whole roof burned off. We were all right, but we didn't have a roof over our heads.
Julia: How did you manage to continue to stay there?
Lisa: It was a bit of a blow, but we didn't give up. We bought an old caravan for £25 and lived in that for a time, while we were doing the place up again, but that got a bit tricky after the second child was born, what with fetching water from the spring and all. So we found an old pub in a local village and lived in that for a few years. It only cost £1500, which we didn't have, but we got a mortgage somehow or other. I had another two children there.
    Our dream all this time was to do the old place up and live in it. It was so quiet. It was a bit boggy, but quiet. My husband got a mechanical digger once and dug a ditch by the side of the two-mile track that led to it, to drain off the water on the roadway. Every time we went there, we had to take an axe to clear away the fallen trees. The rabbits were coming back then and were all over the road. I remember a friend of my husband's standing up through the sliding roof of our old Beetle and blasting away at them with a shotgun. He didn't hit anything though, which was good because we were effectively vegetarians. Whenever we had guests, we used to give them bread and cheese and tomatoes.

Julia: So how did you start on the improvements?
Lisa: Well, we finally got planning permission to build our ideal house there. We got architects in on it. It was going to be wonderful. The ecology thing was just getting going then, and I had been working in a chicken factory for a while and had turned vegetarian for good. If you had seen the things I saw, you would too.
Julia: Then the two things came together, vegetarianism and ecology?
Lisa: Yes. I have to admit that it was my husband really. He really was a bit of a nut. We had it all planned. We would only need to chop down three or four of the enormous trees that surrounded our small cottage, and that would let enough sunlight through to power the solar panels that we were going to build into our roof. We didn't need triple glazing or any of that, because we kept the windows small, deliberately, to conserve heat, so that we didn't really notice the sound of the military aircraft flying low overhead or the rumble of trucks on the M6 motorway just down the hill.
Julia: What other changes did you have in mind?
Lisa: Well, of course, we weren't connected to the sewage system, and my husband had planned a really efficient cesspit so we would be able to use the methane gas it gave off to heat the house in winter. Even though the woods were full of dead trees, we didn't think it right to burn the wood just to heat our house!
Julia: You mentioned that there was no piped water to the house. How did you get over that problem?
Lisa: The water from the well was really pure, and even in the drought of 1976 it didn't dry up. It tasted wonderful. My real problem was to stop my little children spitting in it. So we wanted to cover it over and build a windmill to pump water to the house. There wasn't a lot of wind there, actually, except in winter, but we might have been able to use solar power in summer.

It was an ideal home. Idyllic, really. An old Roman road ran right past our caravan and into the part where the wood got really dense. No one looked after the wood at all and it was reverting to primeval swamp. You could even pick sphagnum moss there.
Julia: How long did it take you to complete all your plans?
Lisa: Well, although we had planning permission to develop the site, we didn't have any money. We bought a couple of goats to clear the nettles, and they had just started to get to work, and we had put a temporary corrugated iron roof on the old cottage, and inserted beams to carry the new floor boards, when – my husband ran off to go and live in South Africa.

So there it is. I have my ideal home, and I don't know what to do with it.

Unit 2 Listening script

Back home

When I was back at home I used to have some fun
I used to go straight out when my work was done
And I never went to bed before twelve or one
And I didn't get up until ten . . .

   And so tomorrow
   I'm going to pack my case
   And by Saturday night

I'll be out of this place
And in a few days' time
You ought to see my face
Because I'll be back home again.

Well I don't know anybody in this town
Because I don't leave work until the sun goes down
And after nine o'clock there's no one else around
So I'm always asleep by ten . . .

    And so tomorrow, etc.

During the summer it's much too hot
You can almost die in the heat
During the winter it rains such a lot
That there are rivers in the street
Yeah, I'm going home
Well, as soon as I'm home I'm going to phone my friends
And invite them to a party that'll start at ten
And I'm never going to go away again
After I get back home . . .

    And so tomorrow, etc.

Unit 3   Listening script

Listen to Robert talking about his pet. Read the questions on p. 10 before you listen. Try to answer the questions in note form while you are listening.

Robert: I've always been fascinated by snakes. A lot of people think they're dreadful, slimy things, but in fact touching a snake is like touching silk. They're beautifully smooth and cool.
    Well, when I moved into my new flat there was plenty of space so I decided to buy a boa constrictor. The one I got was just a baby but even so it was about two-and-a-half metres long. She was a wonderful pet . . . there was never any mess and she only needed feeding every two months or so. I bought a huge glass case – rather like a fish tank – to keep her in, but she was quite active and spent most of the time moving about the place. In fact, the only time I shut her in her case was at night because I once woke up to find her curled up in bed beside me!
    She always made my friends nervous . . . I mean, I could never find anyone willing to share the flat with me. In fact, I even advertised in our local paper for someone to share. The advert said something like 'Snake-lover and non-smoker wanted to share a roomy flat with professional guy and a boa constrictor'. You know, I didn't get ONE enquiry! I suppose all the readers must have been smokers!
    I also had problems with girlfriends . . . that is, it was always a bit awkward telling them about having a snake about the place, so I didn't mention it until 'formal introductions' had to be made. I began to look on it as a test of character . . . you know, love me, love my boa constrictor! I must admit that quite a few never came back again!
    Anyway, I had to give her to the zoo in the end. I'd kept her for three

years and she'd grown quite a lot . . . but that wasn't the real the problem. What I really couldn't stand was having to feed her. I mean, in the beginning I could just go to the local pet shop and buy a couple of mice or the occasional rat – you see, they have to have live food. They wouldn't cast a second glance at a T-bone steak! Well, when the owner of the pet shop discovered what I was doing with the mice, he refused to sell me any more. In fact, that happened at two pet shops. So I was faced with the problem of breeding my own mice or finding alternative supplies. And the local paper provided what I thought was the perfect solution. I started to answer ads offering kittens free to anyone who'd give them a good home.

So, off I would go and there would be a dear old lady fussing over her cat and a basketful of kittens. I'd ask for two, and she'd lift up a little creature and say, 'Why don't you take this lovely little grey one? She's so lively, plenty of character, and what about this black and white one? They always play together.'

Well, you can imagine that by the time I got them home I was feeling a bit emotional to say the least. I couldn't stay at home while she was feeding, so I used to drop the kittens into the glass case and dash out to the pub. By the time I got back she would have eaten them, thank goodness!

Unit 4   Listening script I

Presenter: Lucy, you spent three months of 1985 working as a Venturer with Operation Raleigh. How did you become interested in the project?
Lucy: It was really the previous project that had caught my imagination. That was Operation Drake which took place in 1978 and lasted two years. It sounded so exciting!
Presenter: How did it get started?
Lucy: I think the idea originally came from the Prince of Wales. A worldwide series of expeditions was organised and led by Colonel John Blashford-Snell, the explorer, and an international team of experts. I believe the Venturers came from twenty-seven countries.
Presenter: What was the purpose of the expeditions and could anybody join?
Lucy: No, there was an age limit and I was too young to join Operation Drake. People had to be between 17 and 24 and had to undergo a rigorous selection procedure. The expeditions provided opportunities for young people to work together on projects of high adventure. The aim was to help communities in need, or countries in need, and carry out scientific research. On a personal level it was hoped that Venturers would increase their awareness of the needs of others, improve their self-confidence . . . it was also meant to help them find out about themselves.
Presenter: How did Operation Raleigh come about then?
Lucy: It was again an idea from Prince Charles. He suggested setting up another project along similar lines but on a much greater scale. He proposed an increase to 4000 young explorers and a time span of four years instead of two. Operation Raleigh is the result and consists of a series of 40 expeditions to be carried out between 1984 and 1989. Of course I was delighted because it meant I was then the right age to apply . . . and was one of the lucky ones who passed the selection tests.
Presenter: Why did it take so long to get Operation Raleigh off the ground – almost four years?
Lucy: It was the sheer size of the operation. It took over three years to plan and

organise it. Over fifty countries have been involved this time and thousands of volunteers are still working on preparations all over the world.
Presenter: How long do the Venturers spend on the project?
Lucy: Somewhere between two and three months. The conditions are usually pretty uncomfortable and work is often very hard indeed. They can be anywhere from high mountains to very hot jungles to desert areas, and the Venturers are expected to carry out their tasks – whatever they may be – in these difficult conditions and to the best of their ability.

Unit 4 Listening script II

Presenter: Lucy, you spent three months as a Venturer working on a project in South America. What made you decide on South America?
Lucy: Well, I speak Spanish fluently and I wanted to go somewhere where my language skills could be useful.
Presenter: Where exactly did you go?
Lucy: A place called Puerto Bermudez in Peru. There were three projects in Peru and I opted for Puerto Bermudez where they were building a hovercraft ramp and giving medical aid to the Campa Indians deep in the jungle, but it wasn't an easy choice.
Presenter: How did you get there?
Lucy: We flew to Lima and spent four days at H.Q. negotiating over materials for the ramp. I was needed as an interpreter – in fact my primary function was just that for the whole of the three months. Then we were finally on our way! But the journey to Puerto Bermudez itself was an adventure . . . it took three days. We had to . . . right from the start we had to get used to what is known as the 'Peruvian factor' . . . delays. We were held up a whole day waiting for a pass to be issued by the army barracks at La Merced which was on the way.
Presenter: And once you got there, where did you live?
Lucy: It was a building called the 'camal'. One day it will be the local slaughterhouse, depending upon when the necessary funds are available to put the finishing touches to it.
  Anyway, we set up camp there and within three days had running water, showers, a dining room, an indoor and an outdoor toilet (great for an all-over tan!), changing rooms and a verandah where we hung our hammocks.
Presenter: Once that had been set up, how did you organise the building work?
Lucy: We had a roster. We worked in teams on three-day stints doing cooking and cleaning-up or building work.
  We used to start at 5.30 in the morning and work through the day until six. We needed frequent fluid breaks because of the heat, and food breaks, of course. The teams worked alternate two-hour shifts which often went on until 10 o'clock at night if we were laying sections of cement.
Presenter: It was obviously physically very hard work. What other problems were there?
Lucy: Well, there were the usual insects that are normally found in hot areas and near water, most of the locals had fleas which we all caught and several of the team had tapeworms. It sounds dreadful, I know, but we honestly didn't mind. It was just something we had to put up with.
Presenter: How did you get on with the local people?
Lucy: They were wonderful! They really appreciated our building the ramp so that the hovercraft could get supplies to the village and they all came along

to lend a hand in some way – even just to bring us a loaf of bread from the village bakery. Some of the women organised two pig roasts and we had three birthdays to celebrate, all with help from the locals.

Presenter: Was the village very primitive?

Lucy: Yes, fairly. There was a local doctor and a dentist of sorts, but no medical facilities. One of our group was a dentist but there was no equipment or electric power to do any drilling or filling. I'm afraid all he could do was pull teeth out, without anaesthetic, mostly. The village people just couldn't afford to pay.

They had succeeded in getting running water into several houses, so the sanitation wasn't bad.

Presenter: You mentioned getting medical aid to the Campa Indians. How was that organised?

Lucy: I had to go on several two- or three-day excursions by hovercraft. Once we were invited to a huge meeting of the Campa chiefs. It gave us a golden opportunity to talk to them all and find out what they really needed. I was interpreting from English to Spanish then someone else translated from Spanish to Campa.

Presenter: What did they ask for?

Lucy: Oh, the usual medical supplies, but what surprised us was a request for books and pencils for their children. It seems that a lot of them didn't attend school simply because they couldn't afford such things as pencils. We also did a lot of vaccinating and giving simple medical treatment.

Presenter: It sounds like an unforgettable experience.

Lucy: It certainly was. It really taught me a lot about myself and how to get on with people. I think I'm much more confident and independent now, and the big bonus is having so many very close friends. All of our group became like a family.

Presenter: Would you like to go on another project of this kind?

Lucy: Definitely. In fact I've applied to become a project leader as soon as my studies are finished.

Presenter: Lucy, thank you and the best of luck!

Unit 5   Listening script

(Telephone ringing tone)

Receptionist: Friendship Computer Dating Agency. Good morning!

Caller: Hello. I'd like some information about your agency, please.

Receptionist: One moment please. I'll put you through.

Secretary: Good morning, how can I help you?

Caller: I'm calling to get some information about your agency.

Secretary: The Friendship Computer Agency is an organisation that people join in order to make contact with others with similar interests. We are a well-established organisation and people can join by filling in a very detailed questionnaire about themselves and the type of person they wish to meet.

Caller: And what does it cost?

Secretary: £75.00 per year. For that we supply six names, addresses and telephone numbers and we also put you on lists for other people, of course.

Caller: What if I didn't like any of the six . . . what then?

Secretary: We'd send you a further selection of names from our Databank.

Caller: Do you have any means of screening the people who apply for membership?

Secretary: We have over 35000 members and in the region of 2500 new people joining us each month. There's no screening except through the very detailed questionnaires. We also find the high membership fee excludes a lot of people. We've been in existence for over twenty years and we haven't had a complaint.
Caller: Well, what kind of people do you normally have?
Secretary: Oh, everything from politicians, actresses right across a range to dustmen.
Caller: I see.
Secretary: Would you like me to send you some information and a questionnaire?
Caller: Yes, please.
Secretary: Would you give me your name and address, please and can I ask you your age?
(Fade out)

Unit 6 Listening script

Presenter: People marry for love . . . or do they? The traditionalists continue to have children and settle down into satisfying but unspectacular partnerships. However, the pattern may be changing with the arrival of the working wife and women who are quite happy to see life in terms of practical benefits such as financial security or having a husband who stays at home.
  Lisa is a doctor: her husband, Anthony, a tall, good-looking man with copper-coloured hair, describes himself as a do-it-yourself enthusiast, but adds that he is tempted to put 'house husband' on his next passport.
Lisa: It's all quite simple. I go out to work because I'm better at working than Anthony is. Also, I've had a very expensive education and training which I don't want to waste. You could say the country has an investment in me. Besides, I can earn more money.
Presenter: Lisa in fact earns around £15,000 a year – more if she takes private clinics. But how does Anthony feel about it? Does he mind the fact that his wife goes out to work and he doesn't?
Lisa: Anthony may not go out to work, but work be certainly does. He does the shopping, cooking and cleaning. He takes our two daughters to school and picks them up in the afternoon. Then he makes their tea and gets dinner ready for the two of us when I return from the surgery. Not only that, he's done wonders in the house. His contribution to our family is considerable. We bought this house for £12,000 five years ago, and with the work he has put into it – with only the occasional help of a professional, such as a plumber – it must now be worth around £60,000. He's a dreamer, you see, a gentle man. Being at home suits him. He's just not cut out for the discipline of everyday working life. He fiddles around making pottery and things. At college he studied art and design and that's what he's interested in. He does what he's good at . . . and I do what I'm good at.
Presenter: Lisa is very proud of her husband and is clearly satisfied with her life and her home.
Lisa: When we were first married, I had just qualified and Anthony was working with a friend as a sort of partner in a studio. They 'threw' pots and tried to sell them, and then they set up a sort of weaving section for ethnic cloth. They had a marvellous time playing about but they never made any money

and they were just hopeless about business . . . But, of course, when I became pregnant with the twins, Anthony's studio days were over. I was at home for a year with the babies and Anthony got a proper job, working in an antique shop. Oh, how he hated it – the hours, the discipline, the people. And I hated being at home. Nobody expects a male doctor to stay at home with the children – so why should I be expected to either? And then I hit on the idea of Anthony staying at home and me going back to work, full time. Well, it was logical, wasn't it? And he simply jumped at it! So he set up a studio here, in what used to be the butler's pantry, and now he bangs away perfectly happily making curtain rails and bedheads as we need them. This place was practically falling down when we moved in, you know, though you'd scarcely believe it to look at it now.

Another bonus, of course, about our arrangement is that my earnings pay all the running costs, but his work has given us an opportunity to get some real capital behind us.

I tell you . . . for Anthony, home is heaven on earth. He is doing what he wants, and for the first time in our married life, we have no money worries. Can't be bad. He's talking about making a swimming pool now.

Presenter: Now listen to Frances.
Frances: My work is my life. For a long time, marriage simply didn't enter my scheme of things at all – I'd been far too busy fighting to get what I wanted – which was to be a lawyer. To me, marriage seemed like going to jail, with the husband as prison governor and the children as warders. Has it ever occurred to you how much useless work the average woman puts in, nurturing other people's needs and wants? She completely sublimates her own existence to theirs. It's as if she isn't anybody herself. Well, that wasn't for me . . . Anyway, then I met Charles. I was thirty-one at the time. He came to consult our firm on business, and he rang up the next day and invited me out to lunch. After our sixth meeting, he asked me to marry him. I was stunned. I've been married to him for ten years now. Nowadays, of course, if a girl wants to be a lawyer, it's considered quite normal, but in my day girls who wanted to be lawyers were encouraged to think about becoming teachers instead 'because it will fit in better when you're married'. Really! (laugh).
Presenter: Frances and Charles (who at fifty is nine years older than his wife) live in an enviable London flat. Charles is a hard-working entrepreneur who spends weeks abroad each year. They have no children.
Frances: When Charles proposed I had my own flat, a small cottage at the seaside and a car. Men are supposed to provide all that, I understand. Certainly when they do, they seem to think it enhances their status in some way. Well, I did it all for myself with more obstacles in my way than the average male ever encounters. I felt better than them. I had every reason to.
Presenter: Had it taken her long, I wondered, to decide whether or not to marry Charles?
Frances: Well, I couldn't make up my mind at first. There was such a lot to give up. I had to acknowledge, though, that Charles was different from most of the other men I'd met – persistent and absolutely irrepressible about the idea of us getting married.

I found it quite endearing. He's certainly not good looking, but he does have charisma – that's important. I suppose he wore me down in the end . . . One thing's for sure: I'd never have just lived with him. That really is a mug's game and any woman who thinks it's freedom has succumbed to the con trick of the century.

In the end Charles and I made a contract. We would try marriage for a year and if, on our first wedding anniversary, it wasn't working then I'd just go back to my flat, and we'd forget the whole thing. No alimony, no recriminations.
Presenter: What about romance? I suggested.

Frances: Actually I'm not a very romantic person and I don't feel the need for company much either.

Our wedding certainly wasn't the least bit romantic. We got married on a Saturday and he went back to work on the Monday. I left my flat with the electric timer switched on and the bed made up, just in case. It was as if I'd left to go out for the day. I cancelled the milk and the papers but I didn't breathe a word to the neighbours. Yes, I was as cautious as that ... And quite rightly too!

However, on our first anniversary we were still together. We drank to the next twelve months. Now we drink to the next twelve years.

Presenter: Why does she feel that her marriage has been a success?

Frances: Charles and I don't live in each other's pockets. That's one of the reasons why it works, I suppose. He also pulls his weight about the flat – he does not divide the work into male and female jobs, you see. He'll happily do the dishes while I deal with the electrician. Then, of course, he's away a lot. I never make a hassle about where and when. We respect each other's work and each other's privacy.

There could never be anybody else for either of us.

No other two people could fit in with our lifestyle, I think. Certainly children couldn't. We've never felt the need for anybody else in our family. It's astonishing, but we talk to each other endlessly, almost as if we'd just met – about politics, the world . . . anything, in fact, but the price of cabbage.

Although Charles is an intensely interesting man to me, he never, never asks my advice on business matters. He simply does not believe that behind every great man there is a little woman urging him on. His view is that if she is there, then she should step forward and do the job herself. That's one of the refreshing things about him. He positively expects a woman to turn in the same sort of working performance as a man.

I don't have a housekeeping allowance. Whoever is around pays the bills when they come in. We go shopping for food together and the first at the checkout pays. Money is no problem because we both earn it – and that's how we want it to stay.

Unit 7   Listening script

Marriage guidance: The wife

Counsellor: Thank you for coming to see us, Mrs Masters. As your solicitors probably explained to you, before you finally decide to go ahead with the divorce it is always good to have time for reflection, and also to have someone to talk your problems over with. Let me assure you that anything you say will go no further than the walls of this office.

Mrs Masters: Oh yes, I wouldn't want that to happen. It would be very embarrasing if he knew what I said.

Counsellor: Yes, of course. But we will be inviting your husband later on to tell us his side of the story, so he has to find out sooner or later.

Mrs Masters: You won't tell him what I say, will you?

Counsellor: Not in so many words. First of all before we get down to details could you tell me a little about yourself? You put down here that you worked in the Town Hall.

Mrs Masters: Yes, I used to be a typist in the town planning department.
Counsellor: And you gave it up when you got married.
Mrs Masters: Not at first, but my husband doesn't think a woman ought to work when she's married.
Counsellor: Now then, Mrs Masters, I think it would be a good idea if we began at the beginning. When did things start to go wrong?
Mrs Masters: Things were all right at first. He was fairly tall and not bad looking. It was a whirlwind romance. We used to go dancing a lot, even though he is six inches shorter than I am. We didn't use to talk much.
Counsellor: What does your husband do?
Mrs Masters: When we got married he was still a student. He had two more years to do so I used to help him out. He didn't have to pay for a room.
Counsellor: And what was he studying?
Mrs Masters: Philosophy mainly, so it wasn't easy for him to get a job when he finished. He spent a year looking round, worked as a postman, on the buses, odd jobs.
Counsellor: Is he out of work still?
Mrs Masters: Oh no, he's got plenty of work now, he works for himself.
Counsellor: Well, what exactly is the problem?
Mrs Masters: The trouble began really when he started work. He became obsessive and stopped looking after himself. We didn't go out dancing any more, we didn't go out at all. I don't know what it was, he just lost interest. He really let himself go, and especially with regard to personal hygiene.
Counsellor: Just how do you mean, Mrs Masters?
Mrs Masters: Well, he completely neglected to cut his toe nails. He let them grow really long. I didn't pay too much attention to this at first, though I could see that it might mean trouble. They were sharp and cut into the bedsheets. I ended up buying sheets by the dozen.
Counsellor: Why didn't you tell him to cut them?
Mrs Masters: Well, I didn't like to at first. Well, you don't, do you? It's kind of personal. I did later, but by then he was paying no attention to me at all so it wouldn't have worked.
Counsellor: Did he never cut his toe nails?
Mrs Masters: Not once in the seven years since he starting working. They've got really grotesque, by now, must be a couple of inches long and curled up under his toes. Horrible.
Counsellor: It must be very difficult for him to wash his feet.
Mrs Masters: Wash? He doesn't wash his feet.
Counsellor: How does he manage to do his work?
Mrs Masters: That's always amazed me. He's a computer programmer of some kind and he doesn't need to go out. He just sits there all day in front of the keyboard and the telephone by his side. He doesn't even watch television. He just stares at this screen all day and most of the night too. He doesn't cut his fingernails, either, but he chews them down so that he can press the keys.
Counsellor: And you say he never goes out?
Mrs Masters: That's right. He just sits there, staring, and reaching out a hand every two minutes to stuff a potato crisps into his mouth. He has boxes of crisps stacked up on one side and boxes of ginger biscuits on the other. That's all he ever does. He just sits there and taps at the keys, going munch, munch.
Counsellor: Have you tried to persuade him to get up and do something different?
Mrs Masters: Oh yes, I tried all things. He did at first. He would get up and shuffle down to the bottom of the garden, and then come in and go back to the keyboard. He was living in a world of his own. I wouldn't really have minded so much, I could have got on with my life, I had somewhere to live, but I cared, or I thought I did, and I kept on trying, until I gave up. No, it

was the smell and the sight of him that so appalled me. I couldn't bear to be in the same house as him.
Counsellor: Do you have any children, Mrs Masters?
Mrs Masters: No, thank goodness.
Counsellor: Well, Mrs Masters there's not a lot that I want to say at this point. I can only recommend that you give the matter a lot of thought before you rush into any hasty decisions, and I will try and meet Mr Masters to hear his side of the marriage. How does he feel about it?
Mrs Masters: You'll have to ask him. Every time I mention it to him he just shrugs his shoulders and carries on.
Counsellor: Goodbye, Mrs Masters, thank you for coming to see us. We'll try to set up a meeting for next week.

Marriage guidance: The husband

Counsellor: Good evening, Mr Masters. I'm glad you agreed to come along and speak to us. You know that your wife is seeking a divorce and we think it is a good idea to attempt a reconciliation before doing anything hasty.
Mr Masters: I'm not so sure.
Counsellor: What do you mean, Mr Masters?
Mr Masters: Well, she will have given you her side of the story, and it will be all twisted, as usual. I've got a list of complaints about her as long as your arm.
Counsellor: Well, I don't want to take sides or listen to complaints, but I would like to hear what you have to say.
Mr Masters: All right, here goes. It is very difficult in the long run to get on with a woman who has an obsession with cleanliness like she does. She doesn't go out to work, she soon gave that up after I finished university. All she does is stay at home and clean the house, even though it is spotless. She is always picking at me, taking my socks off, even though I have only worn them for two days, criticising my appearance.
Counsellor: You say your wife gave up work.
Mr Masters: Yes, she prefers to stay at home and look after the house, though I would like her to get out and meet people. A job would do her good. She gets bored being stuck in the house, and is so listless. She has lost her personality, somehow, become boring herself.
Counsellor: You never go out together?
Mr Masters: No, we don't like the same things. We used to go dancing, but she always complains about being tired these days, so I got fed up asking her. Besides, I have my work to do.
Counsellor: You are a computer programmer?
Mr Masters: Yes, I work from home. But she doesn't appreciate what I do at all. She constantly nags at me for sitting at the computer and earning the money to keep her alive. She keeps on interrupting and telling me to dig the garden or something. She simply doesn't understand that I have to work. It would have been better if she had children.
Counsellor: You objected to having children?
Mr Masters: Not me, *she* objected. I wanted children, not so much for my own sake but for hers. A child would bring her out of herself, get her out of her cocoon.
Counsellor: Who does the cooking?
Mr Masters: That's a sore point. I have to look after myself. She just sits around watching TV and complaining that I don't watch with her.
Counsellor: So you feel that a separation would be the best solution?

Mr Masters: I don't know. I don't want a divorce, but I don't think things can go on like this much longer. She really doesn't appreciate what I do.

Counsellor: Well, Mr Masters, thank you for coming. I'll write up the notes I have taken, and talk it over with two of my colleagues. Next time we would like you to come back together, and we will discuss whether there is any point in attempting reconciliation. We'll see you in a week's time.

Unit 8   Listening script

Parent Problems

We have been taxi drivers for fifteen years and have not taken in a penny.

When our eldest child was only three he went to a French école maternelle, all right, a kindergarten, well, a nursery school. He had to be taken there at eight o'clock in the morning and fetched at twelve. When he was old enough to go to real school the local primary school was just around the corner, but this brought little relief, because he then began piano lessons after school. And he had to be taken there and brought back. A year later his younger brother began piano lessons too – on a different day, of course. Then two years later, their sister began too . . . The second oldest boy began taking lessons on the horn as well. On Saturday mornings. This lasted five years.

When he joined a local orchestra this was just around the corner, so he could walk to rehearsals. But when he also joined the school orchestra, the school was three miles away, the horn in its case was heavy and the bus service unreliable. So who had to take him there and bring him back? He also joined the local wind band which held its rehearsals some way off.

Oh, did I mention the Boy Scouts? Fortunately my lads didn't really take to all that marching about. One day my oldest son was harangued by the lady Scout leader for going there in dirty shoes, so he gave up. I can't blame him. I had been taking him there for about a year, it must have been. A couple of years later my daughter was old enough to go to the Brownies, so she joined a local group, or pack, or whatever they call them, with her girlfriend. Even though it was only half a mile away she had to be accompanied there on dark evenings.

Although we aren't a church-going family my daughter took it into her head for a time to go to mass with her girlfriend. This was on Sunday usually, but she also went on special religious days, Christmas and so on, sometimes to Midnight Mass, and so once again she had to be taken and collected. Thank God she didn't decide to take up horse-riding as well. I couldn't afford it, in any case. I was too busy paying for petrol.

By the time that my son went to music college he was old enough to make his own way there, so that was all right. Oh, and did I mention the karate lessons? Well, actually they were given by a ballet teacher and that's what they were really. They lasted about a year – once a week – until they realised that they weren't going to be taught to leap in the air and kick each other in the face, and gave up. My daughter went to genuine ballet lessons at the same school. Her class was two hours later so we just used to sit around and wait.

Our horn-playing son joined another chamber orchestra, and this used to give occasional concerts in totally inaccessible places, like Croydon or Woolwich. The teachers who organised these concerts usually lived in Croydon or Woolwich, so they were all right. But I had to drive there and back through the sprawl of South London. It's quite fun being a parent, if you are prepared to be a life-long taxi driver as well.

Now the kids are almost grown up. Well, the eldest has just voted for the first time. So they don't need me so much. They have this rock group and piles and piles of gear – keyboards, amplifiers and loudspeakers, stands. Various members of the group have got transport. Old vans mostly. But old vans are known for breaking down, and then it is the midnight phone call from Darlington. 'Dad . . .'

Unit 9   Listening script

A Career in Sound Broadcasting

Interviewer: How old were you when you left school?
Bert: Sixteen, I think.
Interviewer: Did you have O'levels?
Bert: Yes, I had the bare minimum, five, but including maths and English.
Interviewer: When you left, what did you think you were going to do?
Bert: I was going to be a scientist. It was possible to gain further qualifications when you start work, schemes like Day Release, evening classes.
Interviewer: What did you do then when you left school?
Bert: I got a scientific job in a place called the College of Science. I stayed there for approximately five years, I think. It wasn't an apprenticeship. First of all it was on a probationary basis and then as an established Civil Servant. I was a laboratory assistant. I studied chemistry while I was working, and chemistry, physics and mathematics at day release classes. During that period I gained an A-level in physics, failed all the rest.
    I didn't like it particularly, it was boring, basically.
Interviewer: Was it well paid?
Bert: No. It depends what you mean. In 1953 I must have been earning about £156 a year. But then you see the whole thing in those days was to avoid doing your National Service, by studying and getting a deferment. But finally they caught up with me, at twenty-one.
Interviewer: Were you sorry about that?
Bert: I don't think I was, really. In a strange sort of way I was glad. But I spent two years in the Royal Air Force.
Interviewer: Did you learn anything?
Bert: Yes I did, yes, I carried on, and took a 21-week trade course and became a Ground Wireless mechanic. That was the first time I got into radio. I'd messed about with recording machines before. They weren't tape machines then. At the laboratory they had wire recorders. Editing by knots. If the wire broke you just tied a knot in it and carried on. Then I went abroad with the RAF and became a Control Room operator at the headquarters of the Middle East Air Forces. We spent all our lives on shift, manning this control room for military communications. So precious little of my knowledge was actually used. It was fun, better than being bored which a lot of people were, because we were kept busy.
Interviewer: What did you do when you were released?
Bert: When I left I hadn't made any plans because I was going back to the College of Science, my job was waiting for me at the laboratory.
    I wasn't entirely happy about going back. I was about to get married and the two years away had made me restless and broadened my horizons. But I didn't make much of an effort to look for anything else. Finally I read an advertisement that the BBC wanted probationary technical assistants.
Interviewer: What was the process like, getting a job?
Bert: Not difficult. With the sort of qualifications that I had by that time, having spent seven years since leaving school doing technical, scientific-type jobs,

and having been trained by the RAF and then having physics A-Level and mathematics.

Interviewer: Was this a senior position?

Bert: You couldn't get any lower than probationary technical assistant. It was a basic two-year training. I belonged to the Recording Unit and in those days they still cut discs, gramophone records, and they were used as today people use tape. I learned to do all these things.

Interviewer: How old were you by this time?

Bert: I was twenty-three. I learned the broadcasting trade there. The BBC still give training, they have a policy of training their staff from scratch, as it were, to the degree of ability which is necessary. . . .

Interviewer: Are they still taking on sixteen-year-olds?

Bert: I'm not sure. But the training process is largely the same. They will train them for the jobs they are going to do. The interesting thing was that my income increased by 50% overnight. That was the best bit at the time. The work was quite fascinating, and to know that I was actually working for the BBC, it still is.

Interviewer: Did you meet lots of interesting people?

Bert: I can't say that I met the beautiful, the rich and the famous, not immediately. The life of a probationary technical assistant doesn't rise to that.

Interviewer: And what was your next big move forward, then?

Bert: Achieving the BBC's level of proficiency. I was classified as an engineer. I carried on working in the same department. Tape had come in, disc had almost disappeared. I was working in recording, editing, and also manning various BBC control rooms. The BBC control room is very important – you are controlling the whole business of how signals get from A to B within the organisation. It's a great responsibility.

Interviewer: Did you always work in London?

Bert: No, I applied for a secondment overseas. In those days – we're talking about the '50s – the BBC were in the business of assisting developing countries across the world to develop their own broadcasting. I applied for East Africa. This was before full independence. They had a broadcasting station already but the country was expanding and it was decided that they wanted to expand their broadcasting. Maintenance and operations was what I was involved in, mainly operations.

Interviewer: Where were you based?

Bert: On the coast a beautiful spot, typically sub-tropical, quite wonderful. We were there for two-and-a-half years. I stayed on to help broadcast the Independence celebrations which lasted a fortnight, an incredible number of all kinds of celebrations.

There were two of us as station engineers. The other chap saw to the transmission side and I looked after the microphone side. So that's how I developed skills and techniques in outside broadcasting. It was fascinating for me to go to the other side of the world and live in a different culture. It's a great experience.

Interviewer: Were you sorry to come back to England?

Bert: Not really. I spent a short period back at the BBC Training Department and then a vacancy occurred in Sound Outside Broadcasting, and I transferred. I was very specifically interested in the sound part of broadcasting and not in TV.

Interviewer: What would you say was the high point of your career?

Bert: I don't think there is any doubt that the single most exciting event that I have worked on is the outside broadcast of the visit of the Pope to Canterbury Cathedral, it was a unique historical event with a lot of interesting pageantry and all that sort of thing. It was also technically challenging, as big an OB that I personally had worked on, it was an important large-scale operation, and I got a lot of satisfaction from it.

Interviewer: What do you like doing best, what kind of recording?

Bert: Being involved in music, almost any kind. All broadcasting creates very specific problems and challenges, which, if you can crack them produce satisfaction. In the sort of job that I do I am really seeking satisfaction from doing it and if you are interested you can probably get it from music more readily than any other type. Some people are involved in drama, so that's what turns them on, and some people are involved in sport, and that's what turns them on, but I like to be involved in music.

Interviewer: Would you recommend this to young people as a career?

Bert: Yes, provided that they were interested and provided that they could handle the rather odd working conditions, being available for work seven days a week. I mean they don't actually have to put all those hours in but they have to be on call. We work the same number of hours as other people but those hours can be any time of the night or day, any day of the week.

Unit 11   Listening script

A home-worker

There are thousands of women everywhere who are being exploited as cheap labour. This practice began a very long time ago and is still alive and well today.

Listen to Ruki, a former home-worker:

My mother was here, and this is what made me think that I would have the spare time. We were desperate for money, three children and all under five. Ivan was just a year old. And I used to go through the papers and look at all sorts of things that I could do at home, mushroom growing, addressing envelopes.

But sewing, I liked sewing anyway. I used to do the children's dresses and so always I would look out for these things with 'Machinists Wanted'. I used to phone and they would say 'Have you done this sort of sewing before?' At first I was quite honest . . . I used to say I used to do the children's sewing but I hadn't done any of this kind. Then 'Have you got an industrial machine?' These are large powerful machines, they can do all sorts of things, not like home machines. I didn't say I had one.

Well, one man, I suppose he decided well he'd take the chance, so he came. I was quite panicky because I thought he was going to sort of – I was told that what they do is bring a garment and see how you get on, what your sewing is like, and then decide whether you are the sort they need. And I was under the impression that he was going to stand over your shoulder and watch you, you see, so this scared me a bit because things like fixing zips on skirts, these things, I thought maybe I don't know the real technique, you know, but as it turned out he brought this blouse and left it and went away. One blouse. They were oversized blouses and I had to fix a sort of ruffle in front, lace, it was all ready cut and I only had to do the sewing, bit of binding for the neck, the sleeves, they had no binding, it was all very inferior, very poor material, sides, darts, quite a few things I had to do and I took a lot of trouble over this.

And he came a couple of days later and he said, 'Oh, Mrs Shillam, if my girls did it like this I'd have no problems!' He was quite pleased with the neatness and the trouble I had taken and I thought he thought I had taken too much care. 'You see,' he said, 'I don't supply Marks and Spencer'. He sold to the market, I imagine. I think I took about two or three hours. I remember telling him that I took four hours to do it. He was shocked and said, 'My girls do four in an hour!' I said 'No way, no way' could I do it. Then he produced all these blouses.

I had decided maybe five or six would do for the weekend. Oh, I had to do eight to get a pound. That worked out at about twelve and a half pence a blouse. I don't think I realised it at the beginning, you see and I thought that I can't do more. I couldn't do more than about eight and it was pointless anyway, but he brought this big load, forty-eight of them, something like that. My husband joked and said, 'What, are you coming back next year?' Anyway he left the whole thing and went, and I struggled and struggled, my mother was there and she used to sit and tidy up and tie the knots. We produced some really nice blouses, but I didn't do it for long. I couldn't do it.

I don't know how many others he used. He called them 'My girls'. There was another girl, she had an industrial machine, she did skirts and she thought he gave her enough money. She had her children at school and she had all day. In any case I was able to do it only at night after the children were in bed. We used to be up till about twelve. I couldn't do it during the day since all three were at home. A thing like sewing, needles, pins all round. I didn't have a separate room as such and it was just a living room, so it was difficult while they were around.

This was in 1971, I think, but this other girl I know, the one who does the skirts, is still doing it. She has been doing it for about ten years. She is paid a pound an hour, so she has to work for twenty five hours to make twenty-five pounds. Sometimes her work is faulty and it is sent back. She and her husband have to sit and unpick all her work. She doesn't get paid for that, of course.

Unit 12   Listening script

Dennis has had a variety of jobs since leaving school. Listen to the interview and make notes to answer the questions.

Presenter: Dennis, when did you leave school and what was your first job?
Dennis: 1946. I left in 1946 when I was thirteen. School leaving age was really fourteen then, but I was so fed up that I just didn't go back to school after the Easter holiday. I got myself a job instead.
Presenter: And where was that?
Dennis: The Roundabout Garage in Greenford. It's not there anymore. It's buried somewhere under the motorway now! Anyway, I was taken on as an apprentice mechanic and the wages were £2.00 a week.
Presenter: How long were you there?
Dennis: Six months altogether. It was just after the war and the troops were coming home. Well, there was an agreement that the men's jobs would be guaranteed for two years, and the regular mechanics from the garage had come back . . . So the boss came one afternoon and said he'd have to let me go. Well, I thought, this is charming!
Presenter: What did you do about it?
Dennis: There wasn't much I could do about it, of course, but I'd heard about other people who were in the same boat and I just got on with finding something else.
Presenter: Was it particularly difficult?
Dennis: Not really, but then I might have been just lucky. I spent the next two years at a wallpaper factory until going into the army to do my two years National Service . . . I just missed being sent to Korea, thank God!
Presenter: And when you got out was it possible to get work or did the factory hold your job for you?
Dennis: No, they didn't hold the job because there wasn't a war on. But I did manage to get a nightshift job at a warehouse and stayed for a year until I had a row with the manager and walked out. Luckily I walked right into another job with a heavy engineering firm. That was from 1953 to 1969.

Presenter: Why did you leave after sixteen years?
Dennis: The machines were making me go deaf. The work was really quite dangerous . . . I've got a few nasty scars on my hand and arms . . . and my brother and I both went to work for a Swedish company. Well, it was great! A shorter working week and £5 more in our pay packets every Friday!
Presenter: Was the new work any better – and safer – than the job before?
Dennis: Yes, it wasn't what you would call dangerous at all by comparison. It involved welding plastics. They took me on a month's trial to start with and gave me an extra £1 in my wages after only a week and a half! We used to make all sorts of stuff from plastic handbags to junk jewellery . . . loads of stuff. It wasn't bad at all, and I was there three years before they made me redundant. I think there was some financial problem and they sort of dropped hints in advance, so it wasn't altogether a big surprise.
Presenter: Were you able to find something else fairly soon?
Dennis: Yes, not too long. But I didn't just sit around waiting for something to turn up. I had a friend who was also looking for work, so we joined forces and started moonlighting. I made a bundle because it was all cash in hand, you see.
Presenter: What kind of jobs did you do?
Dennis: Oh, painting and decorating, household repairs, a bit of plumbing . . . you know the sort of thing. I was so well off I was able to buy a big colour television for the wife. And that was after three or four months. It took that long for the employment exchange to come up with another job offer at the Hoover factory. They interviewed me and my brother for a job operating some automatic machines. That was in 1972.
Presenter: Did you get the job?
Dennis: Oh yes, but neither of us liked the work. It was a 3-shift system and we weren't too keen on working nights. It was funny really because every week we'd say to each other, 'Let's give it another fortnight, then we'll leave'. But I was there ten years and suddenly they announced the factory was closing down.
Presenter: What did you think about that?
Dennis: It hit me really hard. I wasn't getting any younger and jobs were few and far between then. It was really the wife that pulled me out of it. She got me to write to loads of places to try to get work. Luckily it didn't take long. I had an interview for a night security job at St Bernards Hospital and was offered the job on the spot. Nothing had come of the other interviews I'd had so I thought I'd better give it a go. That lasted two years.
Presenter: Another redundancy?
Dennis: Afraid so. However, I'd been tipped off so I was busy writing off for jobs long before I was laid off. I was lucky enough to get another job straightaway with the local college and I've been there every since.
Presenter: What would you have done if your job applications had all been unsuccessful?
Dennis: More moonlighting, I suppose. And I was quite prepared to move elsewhere to get work. I've never been one to sit about complaining. You can't afford to let things get you down.

Unit 13 Listening script

The Brighton Bike Ride

One of the most familiar annual sporting events to have caught the popular imagination in the past five years has been the annual London Marathon – or indeed the Brussels, New York or Barcelona Marathons, since there is scarcely a city in the world that does not have its own yearly event for thousands or even tens of thousands who shed their grey-hooded jog suits and strip down to sweat shirts and cut-back athletes' shorts for the serious business of long-distance running.

Where once the people of London's East End turned out to line the streets and cheer on some royal procession, or flocked Up West to support the university élite in the Boat Race, now they fill the streets from Greenwich to Westminster for the most unélitist sport of all, the popular marathon. So much is familiar to us from our TV screens.

But there is one mass sporting event in Britain that has been pushed out of the limelight by the marathon. No TV cameras ever roll for the annual London to Brighton Bike Ride. And yet in numbers of participants it rivals and even outstrips its upstart cousin. The event always starts from Clapham Common – you have to have a vast open space to accommodate 25,000 cyclists before the start. These have all the cheerful camaraderie of true fanatics. Since long before dawn they have been up in their thousands, riding in eerie silence through the London streets, blessedly free of motor traffic, to gather in this South London borough.

Like their running counterparts they come in all shapes and sizes, old and new, from the podgy middle-aged executives, to the lean and mean youngsters with their peaked caps on backwards (why do cyclists do this?) and in tight, tight, long, long shorts and body-hugging satiny shirts bearing their club emblems. These are the serious cyclists who ride their two hundred miles every weekend, braving the traffic, and who think the fifty-odd miles to Brighton a bit of a giggle. But they come all the same because it is the cyclists' annual pilgrimage.

But the event has its joke cyclists too, seven-man bicycles, penny-farthings, boneshakers, uni-cycles. The ride strings out all the way to Brighton. En route, the inhabitants of otherwise lonely villages egg them on or invite them into the church hall for cucumber sandwiches. All the cyclists have the vague ambition of getting to Brighton in the shortest possible time, but this soon gives way to having the best possible time. The last challenge before Brighton is Ditchling Beacon. Although no more than a hill, after fifty miles this looms before the bikers like Mount Everest. Daunting even with fifteen gears, only the most hardened regular cyclists pump their way up this. For the rest, it is a case of walking the bike up to the top in time-honoured ignominy. The front runners are in Brighton in time for late breakfast, the stragglers make it in time for supper. Some never make it beyond the second beckoning watering hole.

Unit 14   Listening script

Presenter: In ancient times, processions and festivals were designed to influence the will of heaven. It was the practice of a Snake tribe in the Punjab to parade an effigy of a snake god through the village to encourage fertility. In other cultures, various animals were ceremonially paraded and often sacrificed for a variety of reasons, each in the hope that the gods would favour the community. It has even been suggested that the game of English football, or soccer, is derived from such events. [Over to] Tom Scofield, historian and football enthusiast . . .

Scofield: Well, after the sacrifice of the divine animal, teams or tribes contended with each other to obtain the sacred head, which would be buried in their own territory to ensure its fertility for another year. If this is so, the processions of victorious football teams, returning to their home grounds with their trophy high over the heads of their overjoyed supporters, have an ancient history behind them.

Presenter: So can the origins of the game be traced, and what sort of history has it had?

Scofield: Games or contests in which two teams, or sides, vied with each other in attempting to push, kick, or otherwise move a ball in opposite directions, have been traced to ancient Egyptian fertility rites, as have other athletic pastimes. A football game was played in China as early as 300 BC.

Presenter: How, then, did the game reach Britain?

Scofield: It's thought likely that the Romans introduced the game to the British during their occupation . . . the Romans of course had adopted the game in the 2nd century BC after they had conquered the Greeks, who played a game something like football that was called 'harpaston'.

Presenter: Wasn't there some similar sport in existence before the arrival of the Romans?

Scofield: Oh, yes, there was a pastime called a melée in ancient and mediaeval Britain where a ball, usually an inflated animal bladder, was advanced usually by kicking, punching, or carrying. It was an extremely violent game . . . a mad scramble really . . . more like all-in wrestling! In fact, football was a most dangerous sport until some rules and regulations were established by the Football Association in 1863.

Presenter: How did the game survive when it was such a hazard?

Scofield: It was linked to the religious festivals of Candlemas Day and Shrove Tuesday, which was to become a great football day in Britain. It was such a popular game that several Royal Edicts were issued by half a dozen monarchs to try to outlaw the sport altogether.

Whole villages used to compete with each other at times when they were supposed to be practising military skills. However, none of these royal bans had the slightest effect. When the law made it difficult to play openly, the sport went underground and secret matches were organised.

Presenter: And with no change in the number of injuries, no doubt!

Scofield: That's right. It wasn't uncommon for people to be killed while playing! There was an incident in 1322, for example. A priest called William de Spalding was wearing an unsheathed knife during a football game. In one tackle for the ball he ran into his friend and killed him by accident.

Presenter: You mentioned Shrove Tuesday as a great football day. Why was it so popular?

Scofield: It was a holiday. Business was suspended and the citizenry gathered for a game that officially began with the mayor making the kick-off. Town played town or parish played parish in these festival games, often involving several hundred men who played for hours until the ball had been kicked into the domain of one side or the other. You know, there are still villages in England where the Shrove Tuesday game is played.

Presenter: Though hopefully without loss of life or limb!

Scofield: Yes, hopefully! Perhaps the best known of these games today is in the village of Bromford. Goal posts are set up at either end of the village some three miles apart. Several hundred people join in the game which lasts most of the day. It's great entertainment!

Unit 15   Listening script

Presenter 1: When first visiting a foreign country or unfamiliar city, the fear of getting lost can be a major concern and everyone has a tale to tell. This true account concerns the city of Birmingham in England, but it could happen equally in any city in the world that has undergone a modernisation and rebuilding programme.

Presenter 2: My two teenage sisters managed to get tickets for a Gemini concert at the National Exhibition Centre, ten miles outside Birmingham. The trouble was, we live in London, not Birmingham, the concert was being held on a schoolday, not the weekend, and it didn't end until 11.30 at night. Since I didn't want them to risk taking a bus at that time into the centre of a strange city, then getting a train back to London and another out to where we lived, and getting home at about 4 am, I volunteered to drive them there. This seemed simpler, cheaper and would avoid their getting lost . . .

The outward journey was uneventful – I drove out on the motorway, dropped them off at the Centre and then drove on into the city where I intended to spend the time seeing a film until I picked them up at 11.30 as arranged.

But, passing through suburb after endless suburb, I began to realise that this was an enormous, totally unfamiliar city which might give me some headaches. As I drove into the centre I had to start thinking about finding a parking place and, spotting a sign pointing to 'The Bull Ring', I made in that direction. I vaguely remembered that this was nothing to do with bull fighting, but was the name given to a large city centre development project and I was certain that I would find a car park there.

Sure enough, I drove up over a ramp into the centre and saw a neon-lit sign saying 'Garage Parking'. After locking my car up I made my way on foot to the exit, carefully noting that the car park closed at 10.30 pm, since I didn't want to risk being locked out. As I left I also took my bearings and saw that the garage was located immediately beneath a skyscraper with a neon-lit sign depicting a red bull in outline.

The Bull Ring centre was a desolate sort of place at 6.30 pm, with few people about apart from a few youths kicking cans in the deserted shopping precinct. The whole thing was on many levels, with flyovers and underpasses for cars, and underground and overhead walkways for pedestrians. It seemed to be circled by an urban motorway, across which I could look back and see the sign to my garage.

I found a cinema which closed at 10 pm, which would give me ample time to get back to the car.

After the film, I walked in the direction of the garage which I had mentally noted, but realised that it was on the other side of the motorway, and that I would have to descend to another level to find a subway to get to it. I located a stairway and went down it, only to find myself in the middle of an enormous bus station, whose existence I had not previously suspected. I made my way across several platforms to another stairway which I climbed up.

When I emerged I found myself in the wrong place again. I could still see the garage but now I was looking down over it, and could see no way of getting to it, short of abseiling down the walls. I stopped two passers-by and asked the way, but even though they were locals they had no idea how to direct me through the maze.

I had appalling visions of my two sisters waiting after the concert for a brother who did not turn up, in the rain, ten miles outside the city. There was no means of getting a message to them. Or else I would have to take a taxi, get them home by train and have to take time off work the next day and pick up the car when the garage reopened.

A patrolling policewoman sent me off on a false trail. By now twenty minutes had elapsed, ten minutes to go before closing time, and I was jogging from staircase to staircase. I found one that looked promising and went down it, only to come out into a deserted market hall. Bounding back up the same staircase, I came out in yet another position, this time below the garage and underneath the motorway. The policewoman popped up again, and advised me that the only sure way of getting there in the four minutes remaining was to climb over the wall onto the motorway flyover and jog along to the garage entrance which we could both see. This I did, and jogging precariously along the one-foot wide strip at the side of the roadway, I made it, panting, just as the manager was about to pull down the roller-gate.

I drove into the concert hall parking area in good time, as the crowds were emerging, and picked up my happy, smiling sisters, blissfully unaware of the human tragedy which had nearly occurred outside.

Unit 16 Listening script

The Great White Hope

One of the greatest pleasures available to British youngsters of the 1930s and 40s was to anticipate the heavy thud of the newspaper falling through the letterbox on a Friday. For this was the day that the comic paper was also delivered. For younger children this would be the *Dandy* or the *Beano* and teenagers could choose between the *Hotspur* or the *Wizard* and one or two others.

Strictly speaking these were not 'comics' at all, but were in fact story magazines, containing one or two complete short stories and two serialised adventure stories. George Orwell carried out a study of these comic papers and complained bitterly that while they were mainly consumed by working-class children, the subject matter was almost invariably concerned with the adventures of the very rich, and the doings of public schoolboys.

The only partial exception to the comic papers' fixation with the British public school came with sport. Here very often we see the poor, unprivileged and uneducated athlete managing to outperform his more well-to-do 'betters' and who, although he cannot afford running shoes and runs barefoot, wins the race and gains the incredulous applause of the spectators.

But the sports writers of the comic paper age had another obsession: this was the search for a white athlete or boxer who could rival or better the performance of the black-skinned competition. These writers echoed the call going back to the beginning of the century for a 'Great White Hope' in heavyweight boxing who would displace the hitherto dominant black American champions.

Looking back at British imperial history they resurrected the legendary and historical African heroes, the warrior kings Chaka and Prester John, and elevated their imagined physical prowess into a threat to the stability of the Empire. For some unaccountable reason, it was constantly drummed into the heads of young British boys that they were physically inferior to African youth.

The search was always successful in these comic book stories, and many a fictional super-champion was produced to allay these writers' strange fears and defeat the African challenge on the sports field and off it.

But the reality was different.

The heavyweight boxing championships of the 1920s and 30s saw the total domination of the legendary 'Brown Bomber', Joe Louis, and in athletics, his counterpart was Jesse Owens, the winner of five gold medals at the 1936 Olympics. As Jesse Owens registered triumph after triumph in Berlin, the discomfiture of the comic-paper mind of the German dictator became increasingly evident and, as each medal ceremony came, Hitler ostentatiously turned his back and left the stadium.

Since then, African and American blacks have made certain events their own: boxing, the sprint and field events in athletics, basketball, and many other sports. And what have the effects of this been?

It has taken eight decades of participation of non-whites in sports events of all kinds and at all levels, for the world to mature and come to recognise that this has no greater political significance – and that winning a championship does not mean winning the world or destroying empires. For a Third World country, overburdened by debt, famine and a multitude of economic and political problems, the triumph of its sportsmen is a crucial restatement and affirmation of a healthy national pride.

Unit 17 Listening script

Presenter: In many parts of the world men are taking on a greater share of duties around the house. While their wives go out to work and earn the daily bread, the men stay at home and bake it. But is this practice of exchanging roles accepted without question? Listen to this interview with Leslie Woodstock from Sheffield and decide for yourself:

Interviewer: Leslie Woodstock, your wife goes out to work and you stay at home to look after the house. What made you decide to exchange roles like this?

Woodstock: We didn't decide – she had a job and I didn't, simple as that.

Interviewer: What does your wife do?

Woodstock: She is a croupier in a local casino. So she is actually at home during the day but sleeps most of the time.

Interviewer: And what are you by profession?

Woodstock: An archaeologist. There isn't a lot of work about, and even when I go on a dig I only make pocket money.

Interviewer: And how do you like working at home?

Woodstock: I really love it, actually, though not everything, of course.

Interviewer: Such as?

Woodstock: Well, cleaning, for instance. When my wife takes a couple of weeks off she can go crazy about cleaning and just storms about the house looking for the next thing to scrub. I can't be like that. I tend to push the vacuum cleaner around once a week. I don't mind cleaning windows though, and I don't even mind tackling the really evil jobs, like cleaning out the oven. But I don't get obsessive about cleaning.

Interviewer: Who does the washing?

Woodstock: I do. Well, let's say I put the washing in the machine. I take it out. I go in the garden and hang it out and so on. I do the ironing, too. Just switch the tele on at the same time and that's okay. But for the life of me I can't get the hang of sorting the washing out. There must be something in women's genes. They understand about fabrics from birth, and know whether it goes in at 40 degrees or 90. You should see the mess that comes out if I have to decide: a great clump of pink objects, all lashed together by knotted pyjama legs and sheets. But women seem to know instinctively whether a thing is a coloured or a white or a grey or an in-between. So I stay away from that side of things, I just can't learn it.

Interviewer: If you lived in a place where you had to go to the village fountain to do the washing with all the other women, would you join in?

Woodstock: No chance, absolutely no chance.

Interviewer: What part of the housework do you like doing best?

Woodstock: Oh, cooking, no doubt about it. Being in the kitchen is almost as good as working in the garage. Lots of tools, oil, all sorts of things – I can splash around and be creative.

Interviewer: What do you like making most?

Woodstock: It's got to be omelettes. I can really go to town on them. I love cracking the eggs on the edge of the bowl. I belong to the school which says that the yolks should be separated from the whites and the whites folded in after they've been beaten. That way the omlette is light and fluffy. You don't have to put in flour or baking powder. It rises on its own. I've got this huge chopping board and a Swiss kitchen knife. You should see me go at those onions. No messing about with department store chopping gadgets for me. But I keep it simple – three or four cloves of garlic, a handful of parsley, a dash of paprika powder, some chopped tomatoes. Nothing fancy.

Interviewer: Is there anything you don't like about housework?

Woodstock: When I have made this wonderful omelette – it takes about half a minute to cook in the hot pan and it has to be served immediately – I carry it into the dining room and my wife is somewhere else, anywhere except at the table. By the time she arrives it has collapsed. I tend to shout at her a bit.

Interviewer: What else do you like doing?

Woodstock: Well, barbecueing, of course.

Interviewer: Yes, but barbecueing is always considered a man's job, even when the wife doesn't go out to work.

Woodstock: That's true, but I like it all the same.

Interviewer: Would you consider yourself good at your work?

Woodstock: Well, I would, wouldn't I? I think I'm perfect. I need a lot of praise. I don't always get it. It really irks me that my wife always complains about the mess I make in the kitchen. I admit that I am not the tidiest cook in the world. I can't find it inside myself to wash up as I go along. I suppose it is a bit annoying when I pile all the pans up in the sink and leave them for my wife to clean up (I don't cook and do the washing up as well) and I suppose I do tend to leave rather a lot of grease on the floor, but I do the cooking, after all!

Interviewer: Will you remain a house-husband all your life?

Woodstock: I don't see why not. Of course, if something really interesting came my way, I'd have to take it, it stands to reason.

Interviewer: Thank you, Leslie Woodstock.

Unit 18   Listening script

Presenter: Although there has been such a wave of concern recently about additives in food, the response from British manufacturers has been characteristically slow. However, one of Britain's leading snack manufacturers has just launched a new range of packets for their products. The new packs read 'Free from all colourings and preservatives', so what they've done, among other things, is to remove all artificial colourings from their products solely in response to increasing public reaction against such additives.

A second leading manufacturer has also announced that it intends to do the same thing. But how many others will follow suit? The 'Healthy Eating Programme' has been finding out.

Reporter: 'Ocean Wave' is a food company that has been trading for just five years, but this company owes its success to leaving something *out*. It now supplies all the leading supermarkets with fish free of all artificial colouring. No 'Brown FK' . . . something it is proud of. Simon Aspinall, its Managing Director . . .

Aspinall: Our success, I think, is directly related to the effort we put into removing the colours from fish.

Reporter: Simon Aspinall believes that food without artificial colours is creating a new market . . . one that's here to stay.

Aspinall: This is certainly no flash in the pan. It's here for ever.

Reporter: In Britain there are seventeen artificial dyes permitted in our foods. Colour is added to around half the food we eat each day, and that's about 700 tonnes of artificial colouring in our stomachs every year.

It would seem that the British have a healthy appetite for colours . . . but for how much longer? Several supermarket chains have recently announced their intention to remove *all* additives from their own-brand goods. Why? . . . Tony Campbell of Sureways supermarkets . . .

Campbell: This is purely a response to customer demand. We have customers writing to us, particularly those who have hyperactive children, asking us to please take some of those contentious additives, colourings, preservatives, out of our food.

Reporter: But aren't the supermarkets just exploiting a fashionable fad in order to sell more?

Campbell: I think that if it were just a passing fad, just a PR thing, it would have died a long time ago. No, there's genuine interest. People are becoming more educated. They are taking more interest in the foods they buy, and certainly Sureways customers are telling us what they want.

Reporter: But if we're used to getting food of a particular colour, won't we find it a bit of a shock if it changes overnight? And won't that be a particular problem for manufacturers, cutting out the cosmetics?

Aspinall: This is probably true in the case of such items as smoked haddock . . . er . . . customers who are used to eating smoked haddock are used to seeing it yellow . . . um . . . and that needs an awful lot of getting over.

We, in fact, *have* smoked, and *do* smoke a lot of haddock without any artificial colour at all . . . but it doesn't make the fish the normal lemon-yellow colour that the consumer is used to seeing.

Reporter: For customer appeal, the colour is as important as the design on the packet. And most foods have their makeup done by a cosmetic expert.

But why are we becoming so hostile to glamorised food? Partly it's because of the connection between some additives and allergies, but chiefly because many of us simply don't like the idea of our food being mucked about with. A poll carried out last week revealed that two-thirds of us believe that the use of colour in food is not necessary. Even the snack manufacturers who rely heavily on the appearance of their goods are now being forced to rethink the use of colours.

Ken Burton of the 'Snack, Nut and Crisp Association' . . .

Burton: Snack companies have, in fact, as a result of increased consumer interest in food additives, colours in particular, been reviewing the use of various substances in their products. For example, in the case of potato crisps, at least two of the major manufacturers have made recent announcements that they have phased out the use of colours in their various crisp lines, as well as the anti-oxidants. I think that it is very much a public issue. I think it will certainly continue, and manufacturers will have to respond.

Reporter: So, as manufacturers, perhaps reluctantly, and retailers enthusiastically respond to public pressure, artificial colours may well be on the way out.

But when they're all gone, will we like it?

Unit 19 Listening script

Listen to the following radio interview with a member of the Campaign for Nuclear Disarmament.

Presenter: Dilys, you are a teacher and a member of CND. Could you tell me why you joined the movement and when you joined?

Dilys: Yes . . . in fact I've been interested in the Campaign for Nuclear Disarmament for a very, very long time . . . Even back in the Sixties when I was still at school I had wanted to join. Probably you remember the days of the Aldermaston marches then, but as I was still at school my parents wouldn't let me join. And after that the CND sort of had a very low profile phase . . . um . . . and I was involved in other things, but in 1980 I came back to Britain after being abroad for several years and was really alarmed to find, well, there'd been a change of government. Thatcher had come to power and there was a complete change of scene in Britain. Nuclear war was very much in the air, there was a huge escalation of defence expenditure . . . um . . . Thatcher had a very belligerent attitude towards the Soviet Union and I was really horrified by this. So . . . and CND, I think for about six months before that had started getting much more active and it just seemed, when I returned to Britain in the autumn of 1980, it seemed to me obvious that that's what I had to do. I had to join straightaway. It was offering a voice . . . CND was offering a voice, a channel through which I could express what I felt and make the public more aware.

Presenter: Is this what you hoped to achieve by joining?

Dilys: Um . . . I think I hoped to . . . well, I think one of the issues that was around then, and certainly in the later years was about Cruise missiles. Thatcher was then planning to bring Cruise to Britain and in those early years of the 1980s we wanted to prevent that. We also wanted to stop the escalation of expenditure on nuclear defence and to make the public more aware of what was going on. So in addition to offering a channel of communication to the government, CND was also offering alternative information to the public, and I wanted to be involved for both those reasons.

Presenter: What kind of activities did you take part in?

Dilys: Well, I joined CND both as a national and a local member. A lot of people join their local group and don't bother to join the national movement. As a member of CND I received the newsletter, the journal and kept myself informed and up-to-date on facts, and also went on an annual demonstration and took part in other marches. I used to go, and I still do, to regular meetings where we would have a speaker or indeed a forum having different points of view . . . a Tory MP for example, arguing with somebody from CND. But local groups actually do lots of different things . . . at the meetings you get involved in local activities as well as national demonstrations, go on local marches. For example, last summer . . . August 6th to 10th I think it was . . . every year we commemorate Hiroshima Day and I took part in a 24-hour fast and gave the money I would have spent on meals to Oxfam. We also made paper cranes that we then floated down the river as a reminder of that.

I've also been involved in helping out in the CND Shop which sells lots of goods and books and CND stickers and all sorts of different things, actually. And a street stall in the High Street. Every Saturday there's a street stall with information and various goods that CND sells. So, I'm very involved locally. I've also been involved in writing letters to the local MP.

Presenter: Does the organisation encourage all the members to write to their MP on a regular basis?

Dilys: Oh yes, and to meet the MPs as well . . . I haven't actually done that, and I have to say that there are lots of members who aren't as active as I am. A lot of people don't have time to be so active.

Presenter: You've mentioned taking part in marches and demonstrations. Would you like to tell us about some of the marches you've been involved with?

Dilys: Well, every year now for the past five years, I've been on the October London demo. I've often joined the Easter marches to Molesworth, where there is an American base with Cruise missiles, and to another base at Greenham Common.

Presenter: What's your attitude towards disarmament on a unilateral or multilateral basis?

Dilys: Well, CND believes in all multilateral measures, but I feel that, as most CND people would say, Britain should reject nuclear weapons without waiting for anybody else to do so . . . We should just go ahead and reject them. I mean, the Government is planning to spend £11 billion on new missiles and most of that money will go to America. This escalation worries me and war, nuclear war bunkers and preparations for nuclear war are being talked about more and more, and it feels like before the last war when between 1934 and 1939 spending on the armed services trebled, and I'm afraid that the same kind of thing is happening now. I hate to think about it.

Presenter: Have you yourself participated in any non-violent direct action with the CND?

Dilys: No, I haven't actually, but it's interesting that you should ask that, because I'd like to have done so. I've thought about going on training for it. Of course, you have to be trained not to react violently when a policeman picks you up, I mean, in non-violent direct action you're going to commit acts of civil disobedience such as lying down in the street and you mustn't react at all to anything that's done to you.

Presenter: So why haven't you joined in with any of these activities?

Dilys: Oh, simply because there is great danger of arrest, you're likely to be arrested, and when you go for training they will say this to you. And with my present temporary job situation I can't risk it because it would prejudice prospective employers against me. I have to leave that to other people for the moment.

Presenter: Dilys, thank you very much for talking to us.

Unit 20 Listening script

Famine: Bob Geldof Interview on 'Wogan'

Geldof: It's not glamorous, it's not that glorious, it's something that I wanted to do and I thought it would make 72,000 quid. Events got bigger and bigger and I just stayed with it. And mainly I stayed with it because I said every penny will get there. And unfortunately, every penny got to be over $100 million so I'm still there.

Wogan: So it's Band Aid and Live Aid and we've had Food Aid and now Sport Aid. So, people are prepared to give, but how much money? Is it a bottomless pit that we're pouring our money into?

Geldof: Yes and no. I think the interesting thing is that I thought that maybe we were crisis-orientated, you know, as soon as the pictures went away everyone forgot about it.

Wogan: Well, I must say I thought that you could go to the well once too often, but it doesn't appear to be the case.

Geldof: Exactly. It doesn't, and I think that must frighten a lot of politicians. Now the main reason for Sport Aid is not so much the money, though that's crucial and critical still, but on the day after the Race Against Time on May 25th the UN General Assembly debate for the first time ever the crisis on the continent of Africa and if everyone participates like on July 13th last year they must come out of the building, possibly for the first time in their bloody lives having actually achieved something and they will be listening, they have to listen to quite literally the whole planet doing something again and demanding some sort of coherent action from a bunch of people which we usually expect incoherency from.

Wogan: Talking of coherency, can you put the Sport Aid into some sort of coherent shape for me, because I'm getting confused about what's going on. We have a map over there, we'll go over, explain it to me . . .

Geldof: Well it's May 17th and 25th, there'll be millions of people from the sports world doing these special events, but the main thing which people have to get involved in is this thing called the Race Against Time.

On the 17th a runner leaves the West of the Sudan out here, it's a place called El Abeid which is where a lot of the refugees come from, from the famine and the war, and he lights an Olympic torch from the dying embers of a refugee camp fire, and he'll go to Khartoum, and he'll then fly to Greece, where he'll be met by runners from Mount Olympus and Marathon, who'll add the Olympic flames to his torch.

They'll then go around Eastern Europe to several cities, he'll be met by the Pope and Mitterand here in France, Jaruszelski in Warsaw, he'll come to England, on to Dublin and then one week after leaving the desert and the people who are suffering there he'll arrive in New York and he'll run down First Avenue for his last mile and he'll get to the United Nations Building and he'll put the torch into a giant Olympic torch outside the UN, and a rocket will go off.

At this point, which is 4 o'clock over here in England, all of us in Britain will be standing by as well as all these people from Anchorage in Alaska to Ankara in Turkey, from Banjul and Abidjan and places like that to all over the world. And everyone will be watching their TVs at that point.

Now it's 11 in the morning here, 6 in the morning here, it's 4 in the afternoon here, 2 am here and they'll be running with torches. It's about 1 in the morning over here so all those people will be watching these giant TV screens waiting to run, as soon as the guy lights his flame the world quite literally will be running. Ten kilometres.

It's not much. If you haven't got a form to fill in and send your £5 entry, do it now, they're in all the Woolworths, all the banks, send them down to us, and we're doing a competition through Terry, a one-radio show on the BBC, a one-newspaper, and if you send your form in over the next couple of weeks with your five and just put 'Wogan', just write on it, it'll go into a competition and two people will be drawn out who will fly with me and the runner on Concorde on the 24th to New York and British Airways will pay all the flights and all the hotels and everything like that. So get it from Woolworths or get it from the Post Office or get it from the banks and send them down to us.

The other thing that you have to do is, there's 12 races in Britain, there's 1500 in France and there's 12 official ones in Britain and we know about 400 unofficial ones. If you can't get to an area, an official area, organise your own race, and if you can't organise your own, when you see it on the TV get up, run around your block. If you're old and you find it difficult to walk, make a physical effort to do something.

And believe me, just the pressure that that puts on the creeps who have been meeting here from all over the world will be enough finally to . . . I mean you get your sponsorship for every club, you sponsor your kids, or they sponsor you, you know, get everyone going prior to the race, there'll be workouts with you, there'll be workouts all throughout TV to get you into a bit of shape.

Loads of sports things going on. There's cricket with Viv Richards and David Gower, there's rugby, there's gymnastics, in Birmingham ice skating with Torvill and Dean, Arsenal are doing a whole Sport Out week, there's millions of events, Becker and McEnroe are playing on the Champs Élysées in front of the Eiffel Tower, playing a tennis match. Great.

Wogan: It's got to be, I'm sure and we hope, an even greater success than its predecessors.

Geldof: Well, we're not looking for that, we're just hoping again that people show that they do care, that these people are not going to be allowed to die in misery.